NEW TESTAMENT
GREEK GRAMMAR

NEW TESTAMENT GREEK GRAMMAR

A Course of Self-Help for the Layman

W. E. VINE, M.A.

OLIPHANTS

OLIPHANTS LTD.

1–5 PORTPOOL LANE,
HOLBORN LONDON E.C.1

AUSTRALIA AND NEW ZEALAND

117–119 BURWOOD ROAD
MELBOURNE E.13

SOUTH AFRICA

P.O. BOX 1720, STURK'S BUILDINGS
CAPE TOWN

U.S.A.

ZONDERVAN PUBLISHING HOUSE
1415 LAKE DRIVE S.E.
GRAND RAPIDS, MICHIGAN

This Edition 1965

PRINTED IN GREAT BRITAIN BY
ELLIOTT BROS. AND YEOMAN LTD., SPEKE, LIVERPOOL.

PREFACE

THE production of this Grammar is the outcome of a Class held many years ago in Exeter, for students desirous of acquiring a knowledge of the Greek Testament to avail themselves freely of a course of instruction therein. The method adopted was somewhat of a departure from the rigid order prevailing in the School Grammars. From the commencement use was made of the Greek New Testament, the simpler sentences and phrases being brought into requisition by way of exercises, with a gradual extension according as progress was made in the Grammar itself. The method proved both practicable and interesting.

More recently some of the Lessons in this volume appeared monthly in a Magazine, and it became evident that there is a fairly widespread desire to acquire the knowledge of the New Testament in the original tongue. The provision of Lessons in a Magazine involved their length being adjusted to circumstances of the space required for Magazine articles, and this meant a certain amount of overlapping (without repetition of subject matter from one Lesson to another), it not being possible to divide the subjects so as to put them completely into one Lesson. This, however, did not prove an interference in the course of the study. After some twenty-three lessons had been thus inserted, the Magazine was discontinued, and circumstances, over which the author had no control, have necessitated the publication of the Lessons according to the division previously adopted, but no hindrance to the study is thus presented.

Another result of Magazine work is the somewhat conversational style of guiding the studies and providing explanations, and this again is not without advantage. The student should study the Lessons patiently and thoroughly, and follow closely the advice given as to memorising, and as to repeating certain parts of the Lessons. The Latin proverb " Festina lente " ("Hasten slowly ") is of great importance in this respect, and though constant revision is a laborious task, the ability to read certain parts of the Greek New Testament almost from the commencement of the studies provides interest for those who delight in the Word of God, and makes the task well worth while. The author is hopeful that, in spite of defects, some real contribution may have been made towards this important means of knowing the mind of the Lord.

W. E. VINE, M.A.

BATH

FOREWORD

THERE are many excellent translations of the New Testament from the original Greek into our English tongue, but it is admitted that the student of New Testament Greek has the advantage over the ordinary reader.

The author of this little text book has done a signal service to all who have the linguistic gift. Indeed under its guidance that talent will be discovered and improved. Mr. Vine has long experience in teaching this subject and his Grammar is no mere echo of other text books. His progressive method and the direct use of the Greek New Testament are his own. No better book can be put into the hands of those who have no previous knowledge of learning languages. It is worthy of a place in any " Teach Yourself " series, especially in this revised edition. Designed for the lay reader, it will also find a place in the equipment of others, who wish to feed first-hand upon the Word of God, and give themselves to its glorious ministry.

FRANCIS DAVIDSON

CONTENTS

CONTENTS

INTRODUCTION

It has been well said that the Greek language is "the most subtle and powerful language that ever flowed from the tongue of man." Yet, comparatively speaking, it is easy, and particularly Biblical Greek. The language of the New Testament Greek was much simpler than what is known as Classical Greek, and is to be distinguished from the writings of men who aspire to literary fame. As the late Dr. J. H. Moulton wrote, "The New Testament writers had little idea that they were writing literature. The Holy Ghost spoke absolutely in the language of the people. . . The very grammar and dictionary cry out against men who would allow the Scriptures to appear in any other form than that ' understanded of the people.'" The language spoken throughout the Roman Empire in the first century of this era was Hellenistic Greek, otherwise called the *Koinē*, or the common dialect of the people. How it came about that such

1

a language became universal is described in the writer's manual " B.C. and A.D." or " How the world was prepared for the Gospel," one of the *Witness* manuals. The hand of God is strikingly seen in the national movements which eventually made it possible for the message of eternal life to be conveyed to all nations by means of the unartificial, yet powerful tongue which it is our privilege to study. The study indeed is important as it opens up the mind of God to us as no translation could ever do. Patience and perseverance are required, but the student who has a few hours to spare in the course of a month will soon make progress, and find that he is experiencing a new delight in the intelligent reading of the actual words by which " Men spake from God, being moved by the Holy Ghost " (2 Pet. 1, 21).

LESSON I

The student should familiarise himself with the alphabet, capital and small letters, and their names, and should observe carefully the notes given below. Learn the alphabet by heart; to know the order of the letters is useful for concordance work.

Capitals	Small	Name	English Equivalent
Α	α	alpha	a
Β	β	beta	b
Γ	γ	gamma	g
Δ	δ	delta	d
Ε	ε	epsilon	e (short)
Ζ	ζ	zeta	z (dz)
Η	η	eta	e (long)
Θ	θ	theta	th
Ι	ι	iota	i
Κ	κ	kappa	k
Λ	λ	lambda	l
Μ	μ	mu	m
Ν	ν	nu	n
Ξ	ξ	xi	x
Ο	ο	omicron	o (short)
Π	π	pi	p
Ρ	ρ	rho	r
Σ	σ (ς)	sigma	s
Τ	τ	tau	t
Υ	υ	upsilon	u
Φ	φ	phi	ph
Χ	χ	chi	ch (hard)
Ψ	ψ	psi	ps
Ω	ω	omega	o (long)

NOTES ON THE ALPHABET

(1) There are two forms of the letter E, the short, *epsilon*, pronounced as in "met," the long, *eta*, pronounced as in "mate."

(2) Distinguish the shape of the small letter *eta* from the English "n"; the Greek letter has a long stroke on the right. On the other hand, distinguish the small letter *nu* (the English "n") from the English letter "v." The "v" shape in English is a Greek small "n." The capital *eta* (English long "e") must be distinguished from the English capital H.

(3) There are two forms of the letter O, the short, *omicron*, as in "dot," the long, *omega*, as in "dote" (ŏ and ō).

(4) Distinguish the *xi* (English "x") from the *chi* (English "ch"), sounded hard, as in "Christ." The latter, though it looks like the English "x," combines the two letters c and h.

(5) Distinguish the Greek letter *rho* (English "r") from the English "p." The capital R in Greek is just like the English "P," and the small is somewhat similar. Familiarise the eye in looking at the Greek capital as an "R" not a "P."

(6) There are two forms of the letter "s." One is similar in shape to the English "s," but it is reserved for the end of a word and is never found elsewhere. Greek words ending in the

5

letter " s " must end with the " s " of that shape. Where " s " occurs in the part of a word other than the final letter the other form must be used. It is like an " o " with a horizontal stroke stretching from the top on the right hand side.

(7) There is no dot over the iota.

(8) In writing *upsilon* keep the letter curved, as if it is made like a " v " it will be confounded with the small *nu*.

(9) The small *gamma* must be distinguished from the English " y." The Greek *gamma* is always hard as in " go," not as in " gem."

(10) The student will observe that there is no " h," or rough breathing in the alphabet. Its place is taken by an inverted comma over a letter, thus— ὅς (who). The soft breathing is signified by a comma over the initial vowel, and denotes an absence of the h sound, thus— ἦν (" was "). Therefore the rough breathing or the soft comes over every vowel or diphthong that begins a word. Every word that begins with ρ (*rho*) must have the " h," or rough breathing, over it : thus ῥῆμα (" a word "). When a word begins with two vowels the breathings come over the second letter thus—υἱός (" a son," pronounced *hweos*) and αὐτός ("he," pronounced *owtos*). Double *rho* in the body of a word is written ῤῥ (the first with the smooth breathing, the second with the rough).

(11) Occasionally a vowel has a small iota underneath it, called the iota subscript. This

iota is not pronounced but it is a very important mark to notice, as it often serves to distinguish different forms of the same word.

(12) The *omega* (signifying " great O ") is the last letter in the alphabet. Thus when the Lord says " I am the Alpha and the Omega " (Rev. 22, 13), our English equivalent (though we must not translate it so) would be " I am the A and the Z."

A Table of some Vowel Sounds

α = long and short, as in āh and făt.
{ ε = short only, as in sĕt.
{ η = long only, as in pain (or aim).
{ o = short only, as in pŏt.
{ ω = long only, as in bōne.
ι = long and short, as in polīce and fĭt.
υ = long and short, as in trūe and pŭt.

(*see also p.* 9)

The student should obtain *Nestle's Greek Testament* (small edition) published by the British and Foreign Bible Society, 146 Queen Victoria Street, London, E.C.4. That is the text which will be used in this course.

LESSON II

The following three classes of consonants should be noted particularly,

(1) Labials : π, β, φ.

(2) Gutturals, or palatals : κ, γ, χ.

(3) Dentals : τ, δ, θ.

(a) A labial with s (πς, βς, φς) makes ψ.

(b) A guttural with s (κς, γς, χς) makes ξ.

(c) The dental with s is dropped, but in the case of δς, makes ζ.

(d) The letter ν becomes μ before labials ; thus σύνφημι (lit. together to say, i.e., to agree) becomes σύμφημι. It becomes γ before gutturals ; thus συνχαίρω (to rejoice with) becomes συγχαίρω. It is dropped before σ or ζ; thus συνστρατιώτης (fellow soldier) becomes συστρατιώτης; σύνζυγος (yokefellow) becomes σύζυγος. Before λ, μ, ρ, (which, with ν itself, are called liquids) ν is changed into the same letter ; thus συνλαλέω (to talk with) becomes συλλαλέω; συνμαρτυρέω (to witness with) becomes συμμαρτυρέω.

FURTHER PRONUNCIATIONS

The guttural γ followed by another guttural, κ, γ, χ, is pronounced like the English " ng."

8

Thus ἄγγελος (angel) is pronounced angelos (hard g, not as in the English word "angel," and ἄγκυρα (anchor) is pronounced ang-kura. In the following double vowels pronounce αυ as in "out"; ει as in "height"; ου as in "boot"; αι as in "by"; ευ as in "beauty."

PUNCTUATION

There are four punctuation marks :— the comma (,); the semicolon or colon, expressed by a point above the line (·); the full stop, as in English; the note of interrogation (;). This latter is the same in form as the English semicolon, but must be distinguished from it. The Greek ; is the English ?.

Exercise.—Write the following in Greek characters, without the aid of the Greek text, and correct the result from the text. A good deal of practice can be obtained this way. Avoid trying to learn the meanings of the words. The practice will facilitate progress afterwards. All the vowels are short unless marked long.

John 1, 4.—En autō zōē ēn, kai hē zōē ēn to phōs tōn anthrōpōn, kai to phōs en tē skotia phainei, kai hē skotia auto ou katelaben. Egeneto anthrōpos apestalmenos para Theou, onoma autō Ioanēs. houtos ēlthen eis marturian, hina marturēsē peri tou phōtos, hina pantes pisteusōsin di' autou. Ouk ēn ekeinos to phōs, all' hina marturēsē peri tou phōtos. En to phōs to alēthinon, ho phōtizei panta anthrōpon, erchomenon

9

eis ton kosmon. En tō kosmō ēn, kai ho kosmos di' autou egeneto, kai ho kosmos autou ouk egn. Eis ta idia ēlthen, kai hoi idioi auton ou parelabon.

[Practise transcribing further from the Greek text into English letters and transcribing the latter back into the Greek text.]

INFLECTION signifies the change in the form of words to express variation in meaning. Declension is the system of change in the terminations of nouns, adjectives and pronouns to express different relations, as follows :—

GENDERS — There are three genders, Masculine, Feminine, Neuter. These are not determined as in English by conditions of sex. Names of inanimate objects are of different genders. The terminations of the words are a considerable guide.

NUMBERS — These are two, singular and plural. There is a dual (signifying two) in Greek but it does not occur in the Greek Testament.

CASES — There are five cases : (1) The Nominative, expressing the subject ; (2) the Vocative, used in direct address ; (3) the Accusative, expressing the object of a verb, and used after certain prepositions to express motion towards, etc.; (4) the Genitive, which originally signified motion from and hence separation but afterwards came largely to denote possession. Accordingly it is convenient to associate the

preposition " of " with it. Its range is very
wide ; (5) the Dative signifying the remote
object ; hence the preposition " to " is associated
with it. It also has a large range of meaning,
however, such as rest in, conjunction with, etc.
These details will be considered later.

THE ARTICLE

We are now in a position to consider the
forms of the definite article " the " (there is no
indefinite article " a ").

The following must be learnt by heart, hori-
zontally (masculine, feminine, neuter), and case
by case in the order given. The forms largely
provide a model to the endings of certain noun,
adjective, and pronoun cases, as will be seen
later.

	Singular			
	Masc.	Fem.	Neut.	
Nom.	ὁ	ἡ	τό	(the)
Acc.	τόν	τήν	τό	(the)
Gen.	τοῦ	τῆς	τοῦ	(of the)
Dat.	τῷ	τῇ	τῷ	(to the)

	Plural			
	Masc.	Fem.	Neut.	
Nom.	οἱ	αἱ	τά	(the)
Acc.	τούς	τάς	τά	(the)
Gen.	τῶν	τῶν	τῶν	(of the)
Dat.	τοῖς	ταῖς	τοῖς	(to the)

Note I—The iota under the vowels in the dative singular must be observed carefully ; it is very important. It is called iota subscript.

Note II—The nominative and accusative are always the same in the neuter.

Note III—The genitive plural always ends in ων.

Note IV—Masculine and neuter dative forms are always alike.

THE FIRST DECLENSION

NOUNS

There are three types of inflection of nouns. These are called the Three Declensions. The endings of the First, in the noun form first given, correspond with the feminine form of the article.

FIRST DECLENSION

(1) *Feminine nouns in* -η

πύλη, a gate

Singular			Plural		
Nom.	πύλη,	a gate.	Nom.	πύλαι,	gates.
Voc.	πύλη,	O gate !	Voc.	πύλαι,	O gates !
Acc.	πύλην,	a gate.	Acc.	πύλας,	gates.
Gen.	πύλης,	of a gate.	Gen.	πυλῶν,	of gates.
Dat.	πύλη,	to a gate.	Dat.	πύλαις	to gates.

(Learn the above paradigm by heart, putting the feminine of the article with each case, thus : ἡ πύλη, the gate ; τὴν πύλην, the gate ; τῆς πύλης, of the gate ; etc.)

Declined like πύλη are the following, which should be learnt by heart :

τιμή,	honour	παιδίσκη,	a damsel,	
φωνή,	a voice		maid, or	
ψυχή,	soul, or life		bondwoman.	
στολή,	garment	ὀφειλή,	a debt	
δίκη,	justice	προσευχή,	prayer	
σελήνη,	moon	ὑπακοή,	obedience	
ὀργή,	wrath, anger	παρακοή,	disobedience	
εἰρήνη,	peace	ἀγαθωσύνη,	goodness	

ἐπιστολή,	letter	ἁγιωσύνη,	holiness
κεφαλή,	head	καταλλαγή,	reconcil-
ἀδελφή,	sister		iation.
ἀρχή,	beginning, rule	ὑπερβολή,	abundance,
νύμφη,	bride		excellence
βροχή,	rain	ὑπομονή,	patience

(Write a few of these out in full, on the model of πύλη.)

LESSON III

FIRST DECLENSION NOUNS IN -α
(*These are feminine*)

Note I—When a noun has the stem-ending -α preceded by a vowel or ρ, the singular retains α throughout, as follows :—

βασιλεία, a kingdom

	Singular	Plural
N. & V.	βασιλεία	βασιλείαι
Acc.	βασιλείαν	βασιλείας
Gen.	βασιλείας	βασιλειῶν
Dat.	βασιλείᾳ	βασιλείαις

On the model of this, write out in full
ἡμέρα, a day

Note II—When a noun has the stem-ending -α preceded by a consonant, the α becomes η in the genitive and dative singular (α being kept in the other cases), as follows :—

γλῶσσα, a tongue

	Singular	Plural
N. & V.	γλῶσσα	γλῶσσαι
Acc.	γλῶσσαν	γλώσσας
Gen.	γλώσσης	γλωσσῶν
Dat.	γλώσσῃ	γλώσσαις

Like βασιλεία and ἡμέρα are the following, which should be committed to memory :—

ἀλήθεια,	truth.	ἐξουσία,	power, authority.
ἀδικία,	unrighteousness.		
ἄγνοια,	ignorance.	μαρτυρία,	a witness.
ἀνομία,	iniquity (lit., lawlessness).	σκιά,	a shadow.
		οἰκία,	a house.
ἐργασία,	work, diligence, or gain.	λυχνία,	a lampstand.
		σοφία,	wisdom.
ἐριθεία,	contention, strife.	πέτρα,	a rock.
		θύρα,	a door.

Like γλῶσσα are :—

δόξα,	glory.	θάλασσα,	a sea.
μέριμνα,	a care.	ῥίζα,	a root.

Write out in full, with their different cases and numbers, οἰκία, μέριμνα, and ῥίζα, putting the feminine article with its appropriate cases, singular and plural, before each, and giving the meanings of each case. Do this without referring to the printed lessons and correct your results therefrom : thus, ἡ οἰκία, the house ; τὴν οἰκίαν, the house ; τῆς οἰκίας, of the house, etc.

First Declension Nouns in -ης and -ας

(These are masculine)

Note I—Masculine nouns of the first declension in -ης form the genitive singular in -ου and the vocative in -α. In the other cases they are declined just like πύλη (Lesson II).

Note II—Masculine nouns of the first declension in -ας also form the genitive singular in -ου and the vocative in -α. In other cases they are like βασιλεία (see above).

Note III—The plural is the same throughout in all first declension nouns. Commit the following to memory :—

μαθητής, a disciple

	Singular	Plural
Nom.	μαθητής	μαθηταί
Voc.	μαθητά	μαθηταί
Acc.	μαθητήν	μαθητάς
Gen.	μαθητοῦ	μαθητῶν
Dat.	μαθητῇ	μαθηταῖς

17

νεανίας, a young man

	Singular	Plural
Nom.	νεανίας	νεανίαι
Voc.	νεανία	νεανίαι
Acc.	νεανίαν	νεανίας
Gen.	νεανίου	νεανιῶν
Dat.	νεανίᾳ	νεανίαις

Write these out putting the masculine article ὁ, with its appropriate cases, singular and plural, before each, and the meanings. Correct the result from the above.

Like μαθητής are the following, which should be learnt :—

προφήτης,	a prophet	ἐργάτης,	a labourer
τελώνης,	a publican	ὀφειλέτης,	a debtor
	(tax collector)	ὑπηρέτης	an attendant,
κριτής,	a judge		a servant

THE SECOND DECLENSION—Stem ending -o

Masculine nouns, and a few feminine, in this declension end in -ος. Neuter nouns end in -ον. Learn the following thoroughly. Write them out in full by memory, with the article ὁ for λόγος and τό for ἔργον, and with the meanings.

λόγος, a word

	Singular		Plural	
Nom.	λόγος,	a word	λόγοι,	words
Voc.	λόγε,	O word	λόγοι,	O words
Acc.	λόγον,	a word	λόγους,	words
Gen.	λόγου,	of a word	λόγων,	of words
Dat.	λόγῳ,	to a word	λόγοις,	to words

ἔργον, a work

	Singular	Plural
Nom.	ἔργον	ἔργα
Voc.	ἔργον	ἔργα
Acc.	ἔργον	ἔργα
Gen.	ἔργου	ἔργων
Dat.	ἔργῳ	ἔργοις

Note I—All neuter nouns have the same form in the nominative, vocative, and accusative.

Note II—Observe the iota subscript under the dative singular.

Note III—The masculine article ὁ must go with masculine nouns when " the " comes before, and the neuter τό with neuter nouns.

With the help of a few extra words, some verb forms, and some simple principles, we shall be able at once to read some sentences from the New Testament. The third declension will be reserved till later.

Memorise the following :—

The present tense of the verb " to be "

Singular

1st person, εἰμί,   I am
2nd person, εἶ,   thou art
3rd person, ἐστί(ν), he (she, it, or there) is

Plural

1st person, ἐσμέν,   we are
2nd person, ἐστέ,   ye are
3rd person, εἰσί(ν), they (or there) are

Note—The ν at the end of the 3rd person is used before a vowel, or at the end of a sentence.

Imperfect Tense
Singular

1st person, ἦν   I was
2nd person, ἦσθα,   thou wast
3rd person, ἦν   he (she, it, or there) was

Plural

1st person, ἦμεν,   we were
2nd person, ἦτε,   ye were
3rd person, ἦσαν, they (or there) were

Note—The personal pronouns are included in the verb forms ; they are expressed by separate words only when the pronouns require emphasis.

THE VERB "TO BE"

These will be given later. When there is another subject of the verb the pronoun is, of course, omitted; thus, ἦν ὁ Λόγος is "was the Word."

Learn the following words:— ἐν, in (this preposition is always followed by the dative case; thus ἐν ἀρχῇ, "in (the) beginning"—the omission of the Greek article here will be explained later, it must be rendered in English in this phrase; πρός, towards or with (this is followed by the accusative—thus, πρὸς τὸν Θεόν, "with God," the article is often used with proper names, but must not be rendered in English); ἐκ, of, or out of; καί, and; οὗτος, this (masculine); αὕτη, this (feminine); τοῦτο, this (neuter); οὐ, not (οὐ has two other forms, οὐκ and οὐχ; οὐκ is used when the next word begins with a vowel, and some consonants; οὐχ when the next word begins with an aspirate '); δέ, but, or and;

υἱός,	a son	ἄμπελος,	a vine (fem.)
ἄνθρωπος,	a man	κόσμος,	a world
ὁδός,	a way (fem.)	καθώς,	even as
ἐγώ,	I	οὗτος,	this (masc.)
σύ,	thou	αὕτη,	this (fem.)

Translate into English without referring to the texts (these are supplied to enable students to make their own corrections from the Testament). For the meaning of the words see above.

Ἐν ἀρχῇ ἦν ὁ Λόγος, καὶ ὁ Λόγος ἦν πρὸς τὸν

Θεόν, καὶ Θεὸς ἦν ὁ Λόγος. Οὗτος ἦν ἐν ἀρχῇ πρὸς τὸν Θεόν (John 1, 1–2).

Καὶ αὕτη ἐστὶν ἡ μαρτυρία τοῦ ᾽Ιωάνου (John 1, 19).

Οὗτος ἐστὶν ὁ Υἱός τοῦ Θεοῦ (John 1, 34).

Σὺ εἶ ὁ υἱὸς τοῦ Θεοῦ (John 1, 49).

῟Ην δὲ ἄνθρωπος ἐκ τῶν Φαρισαίων (John 3, 1).

᾽Εγώ εἰμι ἡ ὁδὸς καὶ ἡ ἀλήθεια καὶ ἡ ζωή (John 14, 6).

᾽Εγώ εἰμι ἡ ἄμπελος (John 15, 5).

᾽Εκ τοῦ κόσμου οὐκ εἰσὶν καθὼς ἐγὼ οὐκ εἰμὶ ἐκ τοῦ κόσμου (John 17, 16).

Οὗτος ἐστιν ὁ μαθητής (John 21, 24).

After writing out the English correctly, re-translate the above sentences into Greek, correcting your results from the texts.

LESSON IV

ADJECTIVES AND PRONOUNS CORRESPONDING TO THE FIRST AND SECOND DECLENSIONS

Note—The masculine and neuter endings correspond to the nouns of the second declension (see λόγος and ἔργον, Lesson III); the feminine endings correspond to nouns of the first declension (see πύλη, Lesson II). If the noun forms have been learnt thoroughly the adjectives are easily committed to memory.

FIRST FORM

ἀγαθός, good

Singular

	Masc.	Fem.	Neut.
Nom.	ἀγαθός	ἀγαθή	ἀγαθόν
Voc.	ἀγαθέ	ἀγαθή	ἀγαθόν
Acc.	ἀγαθόν	ἀγαθήν	ἀγαθόν
Gen.	ἀγαθοῦ	ἀγαθῆς	ἀγαθοῦ
Dat.	ἀγαθῷ	ἀγαθῇ	ἀγαθῷ

Plural

N. & V.	ἀγαθοί	ἀγαθαί	ἀγαθά
Acc.	ἀγαθούς	ἀγαθάς	ἀγαθά
Gen.	ἀγαθῶν	ἀγαθῶν	ἀγαθῶν
Dat.	ἀγαθοῖς	ἀγαθαῖς	ἀγαθοῖς

As with the nouns, if the -ος of the masculine is preceded by a vowel or ρ the feminine ends in -α instead of -η and retains it throughout (see βασιλεία, Lesson III). Thus :—

SECOND FORM
ἅγιος, holy
Singular

	Masc.	Fem.	Neut.
Nom.	ἅγιος	ἁγία	ἅγιον
Voc.	ἅγιε	ἁγία	ἅγιον
Acc.	ἅγιον	ἁγίαν	ἅγιον
Gen.	ἁγίου	ἁγίας	ἁγίου
Dat.	ἁγίῳ	ἁγίᾳ	ἁγίῳ

The plural is like that of ἀγαθός.

Write out from memory μικρός, μικρά, μικρόν, "little," remembering the rule about the feminine ending -α after ρ, and correct the result from ἅγιος, ἁγία, ἅγιον, above.

Rule—An adjective agrees with the noun which it qualifies in number, gender and case.

Write out in full, from memory, all the

24

cases and genders, singular and plural, with the meanings, of ὁ δίκαιος ἄνθρωπος, "the just man," and correct the results from the paradigms above. Do the same with ἡ καλὴ ἀγγελία, "the good message," and τὸ καλὸν ἔργον, "the beautiful work."

DEMONSTRATIVE ADJECTIVES AND PRONOUNS

οὗτος, " this " ; ἐκεῖνος, " that."

Note I—The endings, masculine, feminine, and neuter, are practically the same as those of the article, ὁ, ἡ, τό.

Note II—It is important to observe the aspirate over the second vowel in the nominative of the masculine and feminine, singular and plural.

Note III— -αυ- runs through the feminine *except in the genitive plural, which has* -ου-; the neuter plural has -αυ- in the nominative and accusative.

Singular : " this "

	Masc.	Fem.	Neut.
Nom.	οὗτος	αὕτη	τοῦτο
Acc.	τοῦτον	ταύτην	τοῦτο
Gen.	τούτου	ταύτης	τούτου
Dat.	τούτῳ	ταύτῃ	τούτῳ

Plural : " these "

	Masc.	Fem.	Neut.
Nom.	οὗτοι	αὗται	ταῦτα
Acc.	τούτους	ταύτας	ταῦτα
Gen.	τούτων	τούτων	τούτων
Dat.	τούτοις	ταύταις	τούτοις

Singular : " that "

Nom.　ἐκεῖνος　　　ἐκείνη　　　ἐκεῖνο
(Remaining case endings as above)

Plural : " those "

Nom.　ἐκεῖνοι　　　ἐκεῖναι　　　ἐκεῖνα
(and so on as above)

Rule I—οὗτος and ἐκεῖνος agree, in number, gender, case, with the noun which they qualify, and the noun always has the article, which, however, is not translated. Thus οὗτος ὁ ἄνθρωπος is " this man " ; οὗτος ὁ υἱός " this Son " ; ταύτην τὴν ἐντολήν " this commandment " ; ἐν ἐκείνῃ τῇ ὥρᾳ " in that hour."

Rule II—The noun with its article may come first and the adjective οὗτος or ἐκεῖνος after it, without altering the meaning. Thus : either ἡ φωνὴ αὕτη or αὕτη ἡ φωνή is " this voice " (" this sound"). " This Scripture " is either ἡ γραφὴ αὕτη or αὕτη ἡ γραφή. " That disciple " is either κεῖνος ὁ μαθητής or ὁ μαθητὴς ἐκεῖνος.

Rule III—When οὗτος and ἐκεῖνος stand alone, without a noun, they are demonstrative pronouns. Thus οὗτος means " this man," αὕτη " this woman," τοῦτο " this thing," ταῦτα " these things," ἐκεῖνος " that man," ἐκείνη " that woman," ἐκεῖνο " that thing."

Or again they may simply denote " this," " that," " these," " those," when they stand, for instance, as the subject or object of a verb. Thus οὗτός ἐστιν ὁ μαθητής is " this is the disciple " (John 21, 24) ; καὶ αὕτη ἐστὶν ἡ μαρτυρία is " And this is the witness " (John 1, 19).

Learn this vocabulary before doing the exercise, and revise the verb εἰμί (p. 20).

ὥρα, an hour ; ἡμέρα, a day ; ζωή, life ; ἐντολή, a commandment ; ἄνθρωπος, a man ; δοῦλος, a servant ; δικαιοσύνη, righteousness ; δίκαιος, righteous ; κριτής, a judge ; στέφανος, a crown ; ἐκ, from (is followed by the genitive case) ; εἰς, unto or among (takes the accusative case) ; ἐν, in (takes the dative case)..

Exercise—Translate the following sentences, without referring to the Testament, unless necessary. When the English has been written out, translate it back into Greek, correcting the result from the Greek Testament.

Σῶσόν (save) με (me) ἐκ (from) τῆς ὥρας ταύτης . . . ἦλθον (I came) εἰς (unto) τὴν ὥραν ταύτην (John 12, 27) ; αὕτη ἐστὶν ὑμῶν (your) ἡ ὥρα (Luke 22, 53) ; ἐν ταῖς ἡμέραις ταύταις (Luke 24, 18) ; ἐξῆλθεν (went forth) οὖν (therefore) οὗτος ὁ λόγος εἰς (among) τοὺς ἀδελφοὺς ὅτι (that) ὁ μαθητὴς ἐκεῖνος οὐκ (not) ἀποθνήσκει (dies) (John 21, 23) ; οἴδαμεν (we know) ὅτι (that) οὗτός ἐστιν ὁ υἱὸς ἡμῶν (our) (John 9, 20) ; αὕτη δέ ἐστιν ἡ αἰώνιος (eternal) ζωή (John 17, 3), αἰώνιος has the

27

same form in the feminine as the masculine ; ἐν ἐκείνῃ τῇ ἡμέρᾳ (John 14, 20) : οὐχ οὗτός ἐστιν Ἰησοῦς ὁ υἱὸς Ἰωσήφ ; [note the question mark] (John 6, 42) ; οὗτοι οἱ λόγοι πιστοὶ καὶ ἀληθινοί (Rev. 22, 6, the verb εἰσίν " are " is omitted) ; οὗτοι οἱ λόγοι ἀληθινοὶ τοῦ Θεοῦ εἰσιν (Rev. 19, 9) ; καὶ αὕτη ἐστὶν ἡ ἐντολὴ αὐτοῦ (His) (1 John 3, 23) ; ἐν τούτῳ ἡ ἀγάπη τοῦ Θεοῦ τετελείωται (has been perfected) (1 John 2, 5) ; οὗτοι οἱ ἄνθρωποι δοῦλοι τοῦ Θεοῦ τοῦ Ὑψίστου (Most High) εἰσίν (Acts 16, 17) ; ὁ τῆς* δικαιοσύνης στέφανος ὃν (which) ἀποδώσει (shall give) μοι (to me) ὁ κύριος ἐν ἐκείνῃ τῇ ἡμέρᾳ ὁ δίκαιος κριτής (2 Tim. 4, 8).

*This article is not to be translated, as it occurs with an abstract noun. The order " the of righteousness crown " is common in Greek. Note that the subject of a verb (here ὁ κύριος) often comes after it. This has the effect of stressing the subject.

LESSON V

Demonstrative Pronouns (*Continued*)

There is another demonstrative pronoun, the meaning of which is similar to that of οὗτος (Lesson IV). It is ὅδε, ἥδε, τόδε "this" (this one here). It consists simply of the article ὁ, ἡ, τό, with -δε added.

The following demonstrative pronouns should also be noted, all declined like οὗτος:—

(*a*) of quality : τοιοῦτος, τοιαύτη, τοιοῦτο, " such."

(*b*) of quantity : τοσοῦτος, τοσαύτη, τοσοῦτο, " so great."

(*c*) of number : τοσοῦτοι etc., "so many." This is simply the plural of (*b*).

(*d*) of degree : τηλικοῦτος etc., " so very great." This occurs only in 2 Cor. 1, 10 : Heb. 2, 3 : Jas. 3, 4 : Rev. 16, 18.

The Personal Pronoun, Third Person

For the third person, " he, she, it," the Greeks used the adjectival pronoun αὐτός, αὐτή, αὐτό. This is given here because its endings are those of the 1st and 2nd declensions. The student should become thoroughly familiar with the meanings.

Singular

Masc.		Fem.		Neut.	
N.	αὐτός, he	αὐτή,	she	αὐτό,	it
A.	αὐτόν, him	αὐτήν,	her	αὐτό,	it
G.	αὐτοῦ, of him	αὐτῆς,	of her	αὐτοῦ,	of it
	(or his)		(or hers)		(or its)
D.	αὐτῷ, to him	αὐτῇ,	to her	αὐτῷ,	to it

Plural

Masc.		Fem.		Neut.	
N.	αὐτοί, they	αὐταί,	they	αὐτά,	them
A.	αὐτούς, them	αὐτάς,	them	αὐτά,	of them
G.	αὐτῶν, of them	αὐτῶν,	of them	αὐτῶν,	of them
	(their)		(their)		(their)
D.	αὐτοῖς, to them	αὐταῖς,	to them	αὐτοῖς,	to them

Note—Distinguish between αὕτη, this (fem.) and αὐτή, she ; between αὗται, these (fem.) and αὐταί, they (fem.).

Rule—When αὐτός in all its cases is connected with a noun, it becomes a reflexive pronoun and denotes " himself, herself, itself." Thus, Ἰησοῦς αὐτός οὐκ ἐβάπτιζεν, " Jesus Himself baptized not."

Rule—When preceded by the article, αὐτός, in all its cases, means " the same." Thus, ἐν τῇ αὐτῇ γνώμῃ is " in the same judgment " (1 Cor. 1, 10) ; τὸ αὐτό means " the same thing."

Note—We must carefully note the order in which αὐτός occurs with a noun and article, and distinguish the two meanings of the pronoun as

in the two rules just mentioned : for example,
αὐτὸ τὸ Πνεῦμα is " the Spirit Himself," but
τὸ αὐτὸ Πνεῦμα is " the same Spirit." When
αὐτός comes after the article it denotes " the
same."

Before doing the exercise below, learn the
following vocabulary and revise all preceding
vocabularies. Also revise the verb " to be "
(Lesson III).

χάρις	thanks or grace	οὖν	therefore
σπουδή	zeal	ἄλλος	other
καρδία	heart	ἔσω	within
οὐρανός	heaven	μετά	with (takes the genitive ; it is
γάρ	for (never begins a sentence ; usually the second word)		shortened to μετ' before a vowel)
		ὑπό	by (takes the genitive)
πόθεν	whence	δέ	but (never comes first word in the sentence)
ἐρημία	wilderness		
ἄρτος	loaf		

*Exercise—Translate the following, with the help
of the meaning given. Correct your result from
the English Testament. Then re-write your corrected
rendering back into Greek, without looking at the
Exercise, and correct your Greek from the Exercise
afterwards.*

εἶπον (they said) οὖν αὐτῷ Μὴ (not) καὶ (also) σὺ (thou) ἐκ τῶν μαθητῶν αὐτοῦ εἶ ; (John 18, 25) : ἔλεγον (said) οὖν αὐτῷ οἱ ἄλλοι μαθηταί (John 20, 25) : ἦσαν ἔσω οἱ μαθηταὶ αὐτοῦ, καὶ Θωμᾶς (Thomas) μετ' αὐτῶν (v. 26) (this word is not " of them " here, but "them," after the preposition μετά, as it takes the genitive) : Σίμων καὶ (also) αὐτὸς ἐπίστευσεν (believed) (Acts 8, 13) : Δημητρίῳ (to Demetrius) μεμαρτύρηται (it hath been witnessed) ὑπὸ πάντων (all) καὶ ὑπὸ αὐτῆς τῆς ἀληθείας (3 John 12) : καὶ (both) Κύριον αὐτὸν καὶ Χριστὸν ἐποίησεν (hath made) ὁ Θεός, τοῦτον τὸν Ἰησοῦν (Jesus), for the two preceding words see Rule 1 under οὗτος, Lesson IV ; note that the subject of this sentence is ὁ Θεός (Acts 2, 36) : Χάρις δὲ τῷ Θεῷ τῷ διδόντι (the One giving, or putting) τὴν αὐτὴν σπουδὴν . . . ἐν τῇ καρδίᾳ Τίτου (2 Cor. 8, 16) : τῶν γὰρ τοιούτων ἐστὶν ἡ βασιλεία τῶν οὐρανῶν (Matt. 19, 14) : οἱ γὰρ τοιοῦτοι τῷ Κυρίῳ ἡμῶν (our) Χριστῷ οὐ δουλεύουσιν (serve—takes the dative) (Rom. 16, 18) : καὶ λέγουσιν (say) αὐτῷ οἱ μαθηταί, Πόθεν ἡμῖν (to us) ἐν ἐρημίᾳ ἄρτοι τοσοῦτοι . . . ; (Matt. 15, 33).

THE RELATIVE PRONOUN

Note I—The relative pronoun ὅς, ἥ, ὅ, " who, which," has the same form as the endings of οὗτος, αὕτη, τοῦτο, (see last Lesson) and therefore as those of the 1st and 2nd declensions.

RELATIVE PRONOUNS

Note II—Each form has the rough breathing.

Note III—There are certain forms of this pronoun which look exactly like those of the article ὁ, ἡ, τό, but which always have an accent (turning to the left in the text, though turning to the right when put by themselves as below); these must be distinguished; the forms are as follows:—in the singular, the nom., fem. and neut., and the acc. neut.: in the plural, the nom., masc. and fem. For example, ὁ is "the" but ὅ is "which."

Singular

Masc.	Fem.	Neut.
N. ὅς who or that	ἥ ditto	ὅ which
A. ὅν whom or that	ἥν ,,	ὅ which
G. οὗ of whom, or whose	ἧς ,,	οὗ of which
D. ᾧ to whom	ᾗ ,,	ᾧ to which

Plural

(Meanings are the same as in the singular)

N.	οἵ	αἵ	ἅ
A.	οὕς	ἅς	ἅ
G.	ὧν	ὧν	ὧν
D.	οἷς	αἷς	οἷς

Rule I—The Relative Pronoun refers back to some noun or pronoun in another clause, and this latter noun or pronoun is called its antecedent. Thus in οὐδεὶς (no one) γὰρ (for) δύναται (is able) ταῦτα τὰ σημεῖα (these signs) ποιεῖν (to do) ἃ (which) σὺ (thou) ποιεῖς (doest) (John 3, 2), ἃ, the relative, refers back to σημεῖα, the antecedent.

Rule II—Relative pronouns agree with their antecedents in number and usually in gender, but not in case. Thus in ὁ ἀστήρ (the star) ὃν εἶδον (which they saw) . . . προῆγεν (went before) αὐτούς (them) (Matt. 2, 9), ὃν is singular and masculine, in agreement with the antecedent ἀστήρ, but the case differs.

Rule III—The case of a relative pronoun depends (with certain exceptions) upon the part it plays in the clause in which it stands. Thus in the following :— λειτουργὸς (a minister) . . . τῆς σκηνῆς (of the tabernacle) τῆς ἀληθινῆς (the true) ἣν (which) ἔπηξεν (pitched) ὁ Κύριος (the Lord) (Heb. 8, 2), ἣν is in the accusative case because it is the object of the verb ἔπηξεν. Again, in παντὶ (to everyone) . . . ᾧ (to whom) ἐδόθη (has been given) πολύ (much) (Luke 12, 48), ᾧ is necessarily in the dative.

LESSON VI

Possessive Pronouns

These are declined just like adjectives of the first and second declensions (see ἀγαθός, Lesson IV). They are :—

	Masc.	Fem.	Neut.
1st Pers.	ἐμός	ἐμή	ἐμόν, my
	ἡμέτερος	ἡμετέρα	ἡμέτερον, our
2nd Pers.	σός	σή	σόν, thy
	ὑμέτερος	ὑμετέρα	ὑμέτερον, your

For the third person, his, hers, its, theirs, the genitive case (sing. and plur.) of αὐτός, αὐτή, αὐτό, he, she, it, is used (see Lesson V), or the genitive case of the reflexive pronoun ἑαυτοῦ (see below), which signifies " his own," " her own," etc. As to the former, αὐτοῦ (" of him ") is " his," and so with the feminine and neuter. Thus " on his shoulders " is ἐπὶ τοὺς ὤμους αὐτοῦ, lit. " on the shoulders of him " (ὦμος, a shoulder).

Rule—When a noun is qualified by a possessive pronoun or the genitive of a personal pronoun, it has the article. The pronoun αὐτοῦ, αὐτῆς, αὐτοῦ (his, hers, its), or αὐτῶν (their), comes either before the article and noun or after them. Thus " his son " would be either ὁ υἱὸς αὐτοῦ or αὐτοῦ ὁ υἱός. With other possessive pronouns the article may be repeated (see sentences 4 and 5, in the exercise below).

Vocabulary

νεκρός-ά-όν	dead	ἕτοιμος-η-ον ˙	ready
πρεσβύτερος	elder	καιρός	a time
ἀγρός	a field	οὔπω	not yet
ὀφθαλμός	an eye	πάντοτε	always
καρδία	a heart		

Exercise

Translate the following sentences after learning the vocabulary. Correct the result from the English Version (preferably the Revised). Then re-translate from the English into Greek, without referring to the Greek unless necessary, and correct your result from it afterwards.

(1) ὅτι (for) οὗτος ὁ υἱός μου νεκρὸς ἦν (Luke 15, 24).

(2) ἦν δὲ (but, or now) ὁ υἱὸς αὐτοῦ ὁ πρεσβύτερος ἐν ἀγρῷ (Luke 15, 25. Note that this sentence begins with the verb " was," the subject " his son " coming after).

(3) τετύφλωκεν (He hath blinded) αὐτῶν τοὺς

ὀφθαλμοὺς καὶ ἐπώρωσεν (He hath hardened) αὐτῶν τὴν καρδίαν (John 12, 40).

(4) καὶ ἡ κοινωνία (fellowship) δὲ (indeed) ἡ ἡμετέρα . . . μετὰ (with—takes the genitive) τοῦ Υἱοῦ αὐτοῦ Ἰησοῦ Χριστοῦ (" is " is omitted) (1 John 1, 3).

(5) λέγει (saith) οὖν (therefore) αὐτοῖς ὁ Ἰησοῦς, Ὁ καιρὸς ὁ ἐμὸς οὔπω πάρεστιν (is come), ὁ δὲ καιρὸς ὁ ὑμέτερος πάντοτέ ἐστιν ἕτοιμος (John 7, 6).

THE REGULAR VERB

Before taking the third declension nouns, adjectives and pronouns, we shall study the simpler parts of the Regular Verb. A few introductory notes will serve here.

Note I—There are in Greek three *Voices*— (1) *the Active Voice* (as in English), signifying that a person, or thing, does something ; e.g., λύω, I loose : (2) *the Middle Voice* (not used in English, signifying that a person, or thing, does something for or upon himself, or itself (i.e., in self-interest) ; e.g., λύομαι, I loose for myself : (3) *the Passive Voice* (as in English), signifying that an action is done upon a person, or thing ; e.g., λύομαι, I am loosed. This form is the same as the middle in many respects.

Note II—There are five *Moods*—(1) *the*

Indicative, which is used to make an assertion, absolutely, e.g., " I loose " : (2) *the Imperative*, which is used to make a command, e.g., " loose thou " : (3) *the Subjunctive*, which asserts a supposition or condition, e.g., " I may loose " : (4) *the Optative*, used in expressing wishes, and in other ways to be explained later : (5) *the Infinitive*, expressing an act or state, usually rendered by the preposition " to," e.g., " to loose," but often used as a verbal noun, e.g., " the act of loosing."

Note III—There is also a set of verbal adjectives called *Participles*. These are also used as nouns. They will be treated separately.

Note IV—There are six *Tenses* in the Active Voice, signifying the present, past, or future. Most of these six run through all the Moods and Participles. In the Indicative Mood the tenses run as follows :—

1 *Present,*	λύω,	I loose, or I am loosing
2 *Imperfect,*	ἔλυον,	I was loosing
3 *Future,*	λύσω,	I shall loose
4 *Aorist*	ἔλυσα,	I loosed
5 *Perfect,*	λέλυκα,	I have loosed
6 *Pluperfect,*	ἐλελύκειν,	I had loosed

Note V—There are two sorts of verbs, which come under the heading of *Conjugations*. We shall for some time be occupied only with the First Conjugation, the verbs of which end in -ω, and we shall take the Indicative Mood, completing the others after studying the remaining class of nouns and pronouns. The purpose of this order is to enable the student the more readily to read certain passages of Scripture.

CONJUGATION OF THE VERB IN -ω- ACTIVE VOICE

INDICATIVE MOOD

Introductory Notes

(1) The endings after the stem λυ- should be written out separately and memorised. Then memorise the whole form of the specimen verb.

(2) The characteristic letter of the future tense is the -σ- before the endings, which otherwise are the same as those of the present tense.

(3) The vowel ε- which precedes the imperfect, first aorist and pluperfect forms is called the *Augment* and characterises these tenses as past, or historic.

(4) The initial syllable λε which begins the perfect and pluperfect forms is called a *reduplication*, i.e., a doubling of the syllable.

(5) Note the -σ- in the first aorist, and the characteristic vowel -α- except in the 3rd person singular.

(6) Note the -κ- in the perfect and pluperfect. The endings of the perfect are the same as those of the first aorist.

D

Present Tense

Singular	Plural
λύω, I loose	λύομεν, we loose
λύεις, thou loosest	λύετε, ye loose
λύει, he looses	λύουσι, they loose

Future Tense

λύσω, I shall loose	λύσομεν, we shall loose
λύσεις, thou wilt loose	λύσετε, ye will loose
λύσει, he will loose	λύσουσι, they will loose

Imperfect Tense

ἔλυον, I was loosing	ἐλύομεν, we were loosing
ἔλυες, thou wast loosing	ἐλύετε, ye were loosing
ἔλυε, he was loosing	ἔλυον, they were loosing

First Aorist Tense

ἔλυσα, I loosed	ἐλύσαμεν, we loosed
ἔλυσας, thou loosedst	ἐλύσατε, ye loosed
ἔλυσε, he loosed	ἔλυσαν, they loosed

Perfect Tense

λέλυκα, I have loosed	λελύκαμεν, we have loosed
λέλυκας, thou hast loosed	λελύκατε, ye have ,,
λέλυκε, he has loosed	λελύκασι, they have ,,

Pluperfect Tense

ἐλελύκειν, I had loosed	ἐλελύκειμεν, we had loosed
ἐλελύκεις, thou hadst ,,	ἐλελύκειτε, ye had ,,
ἐλελύκει, he had loosed	ἐλελύκεσαν, they had ,,

THE INDICATIVE ACTIVE

Additional Notes

Note I—Some verbs have a second aorist tense, with tense-endings like those of the imperfect. The meaning is the same as the first aorist.

Note II—As we have observed in ἐστί (or ἐστιν), the letter -ν is added to the 3rd person singular when the word comes last in a sentence, or when the next word begins with a vowel. This -ν is likewise added to the 3rd person plural when it ends in -σι.

LESSON VII

Indicative Mood (*Continued*)

Like λύω are πιστεύω, to believe ; δουλεύω, to
serve ; προφητεύω, to prophesy ; νηστεύω, to fast ;
κελεύω, to command ; βασιλεύω, to reign ; παύω, to
cause to cease ; κλείω, to shut, and others.

The student, who should have learnt the indicative mood of λύω by heart, should write out *all
the tenses* of that mood of " I believe " in English,
in all the persons, singular and plural, and put
the Greek against them from memory, so as to
become thoroughly familiar with the forms ; this
thoroughness will make progress easy.   As an
example of what to do we will give the present
and 1st aorist :—

Present Indicative

I believe	πιστεύω	We believe	πιστεύομεν
Thou believest	πιστεύεις	You believe	πιστεύετε
He believes	πιστεύει	They believe	πιστεύουσι

First Aorist Indicative

I believed	ἐπίστευσα	We believed	ἐπιστεύσαμεν
Thou believedst	ἐπίστευσας	Ye believed	ἐπιστεύσατε
He believed	ἐπίστευσε	They believed	ἐπίστευσαν

(*Write out the whole mood this way, in the right
order of the Tenses*)

The following verbs consist of λύω combined

42

with a preposition :— ἀπολύω, to loose, release, put away ; καταλύω, to destroy. In forming the augment ἐ- for the imperfect, aorist and pluperfect tenses of such compound verbs, the final vowel of the preposition is simply changed to -ε-. Thus the imperfect of ἀπολύω is ἀπέλυον and the aorist is ἀπέλυσα.

Before doing the exercise below, memorise the following vocabulary, and the verbs above at the beginning of this Lesson.

Vocabulary

κύριος	a lord	μέχρι	until
δοῦλος	a servant	θάνατος	death
νῦν	now	ἀλλά	but
ναός	a temple	ἀπό	from
μαθητής	a disciple		

Exercise—Write out a translation of the following without reference to the English Version. Correct your results from the English Testament. Re-write the sentences from the English back into the Greek, without referring to the Greek. Correct your results from the exercise now given.

(1) ὁ κύριος τοῦ δούλου ἐκείνου (see Lesson IV, Rule I) ἀπέλυσεν (1st aorist) αὐτόν (Matt. 18, 27).

(2) Νῦν ἀπολύεις τὸν δοῦλόν σου (Luke 2, 29).

(3) Ἐγὼ καταλύσω τὸν ναὸν τοῦτον (Mark 14, 58).

(4) ἐπίστευσαν εἰς (on) αὐτὸν οἱ μαθηταὶ αὐτοῦ (John 2, 11).

(5) πεπιστεύκατε ὅτι (that) ἐγὼ παρὰ (from) τοῦ Θεοῦ ἐξῆλθον (came out) (John 16, 27).

(6) ἐγὼ πεπίστευκα (perfect tense, as in R.V.) ὅτι σὺ εἶ (see verb " to be ") ὁ Χριστὸς ὁ Υἱὸς τοῦ Θεοῦ (John 11, 27).

(7) ἀλλὰ ἐβασίλευσεν ὁ θάνατος ἀπὸ Ἀδὰμ μέχρι Μωϋσέως (Moses) (Rom. 5, 14)—(the article before θάνατος must not be translated ; an abstract noun often has the article).

(8) καὶ ἐβασίλευσαν μετὰ (with) τοῦ Χριστοῦ (Rev. 20, 4)—(the subject of the sentence is " they " and is included in the verb).

(9) βασιλεύσουσιν (future) μετ' αὐτοῦ (Rev. 20, 6).

Before proceeding further with the other moods of the verb, we shall make easiest headway in the reading of the Testament by taking the remainder of the nouns, adjectives and pronouns.

Previously to learning these the student should thoroughly revise the nouns of the first and second declensions, πύλη (Lesson II), βασιλεία, γλῶσσα, μαθητής, νεανίας, λόγος and ἔργον (Lesson III), the adjectives ἀγαθός and ἅγιος (Lesson IV), and the pronouns οὗτος, ἐκεῖνος, αὐτός (Lesson IV), memorising all that may have been forgotten. This is necessary in order to keep distinct in the mind the forms that follow, and especially the third declension.

SECOND DECLENSION CONTRACTIONS

CONTRACTED
NOUNS AND ADJECTIVES
OF THE SECOND DECLENSION

Note—Contraction means the combining of two distinct vowels to form one vowel sound. There are very few contracted nouns and adjectives, but they must be noted.

Rule I—When the vowel o–, in the final syllable, is preceded by ε or ο in the stem, the two vowels generally contract, forming one vowel sound -ου (to be pronounced as in "boot"). Thus νόος (νό-ος), the mind, becomes νοῦς ; ὀστέον, a bone, becomes ὀστοῦν.

Rule II—When Omega is preceded by ε or ο, they combine to form simply -ω. Thus νόῳ becomes νῷ.

Rule III—The vowels -εη combine to form -η, and the vowels -εα combine to form -η or -α. These are illustrated in the adjectives below.

νοῦς, mind

	Singular		Plural	
Nom.	(νόος)	νοῦς	(νόοι)	νοῖ
Voc.	(νόε)	νοῦ	(νόοι)	νοῖ
Acc.	(νόον)	νοῦν	(νόους)	νοῦς
Gen.	(νόου)	νοῦ	(νόων)	νῶν
Dat.	(νόῳ)	νῷ	(νόοις)	νοῖς

Note—This contraction does not by any means invariably take place. Thus, while ὀστοῦν, a

45

bone, is contracted thus from ὀστέον in John 19, 36, we find ὀστέων instead of ὀστῶν in Heb. 11, 22. (There is no need to learn the neuter paradigm ὀστοῦν).

CONTRACTED ADJECTIVES

χρύσεος, χρυσέα, χρύσεον, golden, becomes χρυσοῦς, χρυσῆ, χρυσοῦν, etc., according to the rules above.

	Singular			Plural		
	M.	F.	N.	M.	F.	N.
N.	χρυσοῦς	χρυσῆ	χρυσοῦν	χρυσοῖ	-αῖ	-ᾶ
[V.	χρύσεε	χρυσῆ	χρυσοῦν]	[χρυσοῖ	-αῖ	-ᾶ]
A.	χρυσοῦν	χρυσῆν	χρυσοῦν	χρυσοῦς	-ᾶς	-ᾶ
G.	χρυσοῦ	χρυσῆς	χρυσοῦ	χρυσῶν	-ῶν	-ῶν
D.	χρυσῷ	χρυσῇ	χρυσῷ	χρυσοῖς	-αῖς	-οῖς

TWO IRREGULAR ADJECTIVES

Note—The following adjectives are important, as they are of very frequent occurrence ; they should be committed to memory. They are irregular only in the masculine and neuter singular, which present shortened forms.

μέγας, great

Singular

	Masc.	Fem.	Neut.
Nom.	μέγας	μεγάλη	μέγα
Acc.	μέγαν	μεγάλην	μέγα
Gen.	μεγάλου	μεγάλης	μεγάλου
Dat.	μεγάλῳ	μεγάλη	μεγάλῳ

THE THIRD DECLENSION

Plural

The plural is regular, as if from μεγάλος, and runs μεγάλοι, μεγάλαι, μεγάλα, etc.

πολύς, many

Singular

	Masc.	Fem.	Neut.
Nom.	πολύς	πολλή	πολύ
Acc.	πολύν	πολλήν	πολύ
Gen.	πολλοῦ	πολλῆς	πολλοῦ
Dat.	πολλῷ	πολλῇ	πολλῷ

Plural

The plural is regular as if from πολλός, and runs πολλοί, πολλαί, πολλά, etc.

THE THIRD DECLENSION

Introductory Note—Nouns in this declension are of all three genders. There is a considerable variety and hence a number of paradigms are necessary, but all follow a simple form which presents little or no difficulty.

The essential thing is to know the *stem*, i.e., the elementary part of the word apart from the endings, or inflections. The stem can always be found from the genitive singular by taking away the inflection ending. Note that the genitive singular in the third declension usually ends in -ος. Take away the -ος and you have the stem.

The stem will be a guide to the nominative case.

We will begin with two simple forms, one of a masculine noun (the feminine would be the same) and one of a neuter noun. When these are learnt, the rest will follow easily.

αἰών, an age (masc.)

stem, αἰών-

	Singular		Plural	
N.	αἰών	an age	αἰῶνες	ages
V.	αἰών	O age	αἰῶνες	,,
A.	αἰῶνα	an age	αἰῶνας	,,
G.	αἰῶνος	of an age	αἰώνων	of ages
D.	αἰῶνι	to an age	αἰῶσι (ν)	to ,,

ῥῆμα, a word (neut.)

stem, ῥηματ-

	Singular	Plural
Nom.	ῥῆμα	ῥήματα
Voc.	ῥῆμα	ῥήματα
Acc.	ῥῆμα	ῥήματα
Ger.	ῥήματος	ῥημάτων
Dat.	ῥήματι	ῥήμασι(ν)

Notes

(1) The nominative and vocative are alike, and in the neuter the accusative also, as in the first and second declensions.

(2) The accusative singular ending -α was originally -ν, as in the other declensions, and the -ν is retained in several third declension nouns,

the stems of which end in a vowel. These will be illustrated later. The -α ending should, however, be regarded as normal.

(3) The genitive singular ending is -ος, added to the stem.

(4) The dative singular ending is -ι, added to the stem.

(5) The nominative plural, in masculine and feminine nouns, ends in -ες, added to the stem. Neuter plurals always end in -α in the nominative, vocative, and accusative.

(6) The accusative plural masculine ends in -ας.

(7) The genitive plural ends in -ων, added to the stem. All genitive plurals end in -ων.

(8) The dative plural ends in -σι, added to the stem, with various modifications. The -ν in brackets in the dative plural does not belong to the word ; it is added at the close of a sentence, or when the next word begins with a vowel ; this is simply for the sake of the sound.

LESSON VIII

THE THIRD DECLENSION (*continued*)

Rule 1—The usual ending of the nominative singular is ς, added to the stem. The nominative endings provide a considerable variety and present a difference in form from that of the stem seen in the other cases. There are certain principles which govern the formation of the nominative, but these need not be learned. They simply serve to show that the variety of the third declension nouns is based on one form of case ending. The student should become familiar with the actual examples given and should keep in memory the other case endings, namely, -α, -ος, -ι, of the singular, and -ας, -ων, -σι, of the plural, as already learned in the noun αἰών.

We will first take the noun κῆρυξ, a herald. The paradigm is as follows :—

	Singular	Plural
Nom.	κῆρυξ	κήρυκες
Voc.	κῆρυξ	κήρυκες
Acc.	κήρυκα	κήρυκας
Gen.	κήρυκος	κηρύκων
Dat.	κήρυκι	κήρυξι

50

THE THIRD DECLENSION

The question arises as to why the nominative, vocative singular, and dative plural have an ξ, whereas the rest of the cases have a κ. The explanation is as follows :—

When the stem (here κήρυκ-) ends in κ, or γ, or χ (which letters are called *gutturals*), the addition of the ς to the stem produces the letter ξ in the nominative and vocative singular and the dative plural. Thus κῆρυκ with ς, makes not κῆρυκς but κῆρυξ. The other cases retain the κ-.

Take another noun with a guttural stem :— In Heb. 1, 8 the student will see the word φλογός. This is a genitive case. Take away the -ος and the stem is φλογ-. The Concordance shows that the nominative is φλόξ. The ξ is due to the combination of the letters γ and ς. So νυκτός (Mark 5, 5) is the genitive of νύξ "might." Write out in full, on the model of κῆρυξ above, φλόξ, φλόγα etc. (dat. plur. φλοξί) and νύξ, νύκτα etc.

We will next take the noun Ἄραψ, an Arab. The paradigm is as follows :—

	Singular	Plural
Nom.	Ἄραψ	Ἄραβες
Voc.	Ἄραψ	Ἄραβες
Acc.	Ἄραβα	Ἄραβας
Gen.	Ἄραβος	Ἀράβων
Dat.	Ἄραβι	Ἄραψι

The stem is seen to be Ἀραβ-. When a stem ends in π, or β, or φ (which letters are called *labials*) the addition of the ς to the stem produces the letter ψ. Thus Ἀραβ- with ς makes, not Ἀραβς, but Ἀραψ.

Now for a third specimen :—In Acts 4, 25, the word παιδός occurs (a genitive case). The Concordance shows that the nominative is παῖς. Take away the -ος and we get the stem παιδ-. The paradigm is as follows :—

	Singular	Plural
Nom.	παῖς	παῖδες
Voc.	παῖς	παῖδες
Acc.	παῖδα	παῖδας
Gen.	παιδός	παίδων
Dat.	παιδί	παισί

We observe that the stem is παιδ-. Now whenever a stem ends in τ, or δ, or θ (which letters are called *dentals*) the addition of ς causes the dropping of the τ, δ, or θ. Hence παιδς becomes παῖς and παιδσι becomes παισί. Similarly ἐλπιδ- is the stem of ἐλπίς, hope. The student should write out ἐλπίς in all its cases from memory, on the model of παῖς.

Note—Nouns in the third declension whose nominative ends in -ις, -υς, -αυς, and -ους usually have, in the accusative singular, a shortened form ending in -ν. Thus while the stem of χάρις, grace (or thanks) is χαριτ-, *and hence the genitive is* χάριτος, *and the dative* χάριτι, *the accusative is* χάριν, *but* χάριτα *exceptionally in Acts* 24, 27.

To take a fourth variety, ἰχθύος is " of a fish.'' Take away the -ος and we get the stem ἰχθυ-. This stem ends, then, in a vowel. When a stem ends in a vowel the nominative is formed by simply adding the ς ; " a fish '' is ἰχθύς.

Bearing in mind the note just given, that the accusative of nouns ending in -υς etc. ends, not in -α, but in -ν, we have the following paradigm for ἰχθύς :—

	Singular	Plural
Nom.	ἰχθύς	ἰχθύες
Voc.	ἰχθύς	ἰχθύες
Acc.	ἰχθύν	ἰχθῦς
Gen.	ἰχθύος	ἰχθύων
Dat.	ἰχθύϊ	ἰχθύσι

Rule 2 (not to be committed to memory)— When a stem ends in -ν, or -ντ, or -ς the nominative is formed by lengthening the preceding vowel. The same is usually the case with a stem ending in -ρ.

Take for example, ποιμεν-, the stem of the word for " a shepherd.'' The nominative is ποιμήν (note the η instead of ε) ; the accusative is ποιμένα, the genitive ποιμένος, etc. Note that the dative plural is ποιμέσι (not ποιμένσι,—the ν was dropped before ς) ; again, λέων, a lion (stem λεοντ-) has accusative λέοντα, genitive λέοντος, etc. The dative plural is λέουσι not λέοντσι—a combination too awkward for Greek ears ; note the ω in the nominative instead of ο. So again with ῥήτωρ, an orator (stem ῥήτορ-), it has accus. ῥήτορα, etc. The dative plural is ῥήτορσι.

Write out the declension of ποιμήν, λέων, and ῥήτωρ in full.

Note—One or two nouns ending in ρ are a little irregular. The two following must be memorised :—

πατήρ, a father

	Singular	Plural
Nom.	πατήρ	πατέρες
Voc.	πάτερ*	πατέρες
Acc.	πατέρα	πατέρας
Gen.	πατρός	πατέρων
Dat.	πατρί	πατράσι

*(Note short ε)

Note—μήτηρ, a mother, and θυγάτηρ, a daughter, are declined in the same way. Write them out in full from memory, not forgetting the shortened form in the gen. and dat. sing., and the gen. plur., and the α in the dat. plural.

THE THIRD DECLENSION

ἀνήρ, a man

	Singular	Plural
Nom.	ἀνήρ	ἄνδρες
Voc.	ἄνερ	ἄνδρες
Acc.	ἄνδρα	ἄνδρας
Gen.	ἀνδρός	ἀνδρῶν
Dat.	ἀνδρί	ἀνδράσι

Note—ἀστήρ, a star, keeps the ε throughout (e.g., gen. ἀστέρος), except that the dative plural is ἀστράσι.

Exercise

Learn the following vocabulary before doing the exercise, and revise the indicative mood of λύω.

λέγω	I say	ἑπτά	seven
τηρέω	I keep	ἀστήρ	star
ποιέω	I do	ὀφθαλμός	eye
πιστεύω	I believe	βίος	life
φανερόω	I manifest	ἀρχή	beginning
κόσμος	world	σημεῖον	sign
ἐπιθυμία	lust	δόξα	glory
σάρξ	flesh	μαθητής	disciple
	(gen. σαρκός)	νύξ	night
διάκονος	a servant	φυλακή	a guard, or watch
καλός-ή-όν	good		
οἶνος	wine	λυχνία	lampstand
ἕως	until	ἀλαζονεία	vainglory
ἄρτι	now		

E

55

Translate, correcting the result from the English Bible, and then re-translate into the Greek :

(1) λέγει ἡ μήτηρ αὐτοῦ τοῖς διακόνοις (John 2, 5).

(2) σὺ τετήρηκας (see τηρέω in the vocabulary above. What tense is indicated by the reduplicating syllable τε- ?) τὸν καλὸν οἶνον ἕως ἄρτι. Ταύτην ἐποίησεν (1st aorist of ποιέω—note the augment ἐ-) ἀρχὴν τῶν σημείων ὁ Ἰησοῦς ἐν Κανᾷ τῆς Γαλιλαίας καὶ ἐφανέρωσεν (1st aorist of φανερόω) τὴν δόξαν αὐτοῦ καὶ ἐπίστευσαν εἰς (on) αὐτὸν οἱ μαθηταὶ αὐτοῦ (John 2, end of verse 10 and 11).

(3) τετάρτῃ ("at the fourth") δὲ φυλακῇ (this is a dative of time—hence the whole phrase is "at [not "to"] the fourth watch") τῆς νυκτὸς ἦλθεν (He came) πρὸς (to) αὐτούς (Matt. 14, 25).

(4) οἱ ἑπτὰ ἀστέρες ἄγγελοι τῶν ἑπτὰ ἐκκλησιῶν εἰσιν, καὶ αἱ λυχνίαι αἱ ἑπτὰ ἑπτὰ ἐκκλησίαι εἰσιν (Rev. 1, 20, end, R.V.).

(5) πεπιστεύκαμεν τὴν ἀγαπην ἣν ἔχει ὁ Θεὸς ἐν ἡμῖν (us) (1 John 4, 16).

(6) Translate 1 John 2, 16, bearing in mind that ὅτι is "for"; πᾶν τό is "all the," i.e., "all that is."

(7) Translate Acts 3, 1 : ἀνέβαινον is the 3rd person plural, imperfect tense of ἀναβαίνω, I go up : the augment is formed by changing the final vowel of the preposition ἀνά "up" to -ε : βαίνω is "I go"; the augment must come immediately before it. This is always the case where a preposition is combined with a verb. ἱερόν,

THE THIRD DECLENSION

" temple " ; ἐπί, " at " ; προσευχή, " prayer " ;
ἐνάτος, " ninth."

(8) Translate John 1, 45 : ἔγραψεν is the 3rd
pers. sing. 1st aorist of γράφω, " I write " ; εὑρήκα-
μεν is the 1st pers. plur. of the perfect of εὑρίσκω,
" I find."

LESSON IX

The Third Declension (*continued*)

Rule 3—Some nouns ending in -ις and -ευς have a genitive ending with -εως instead of -ος. The two following should be memorised :—

πόλις, a city (feminine)

(stem πολι-)

	Singular	Plural	
Nom.	πόλις	πόλεις	(for πόλεες)
Voc.	πόλι	πόλεις	(do.)
Acc.	πόλιν	πόλεις	(for πόλεας)
Gen.	πόλεως	πόλεων	
Dat.	πόλει	πόλεσι	

(*Note the accusative in -ιν ; see note in Lesson VIII*)

Like πόλις are δύναμις, power ; κρίσις, judgment ; ὄφις, a serpent, and others.

βασιλεύς, a king

	Singular	Plural	
Nom.	βασιλεύς	βασιλεῖς	(for βασιλέες)
Voc.	βασιλεῦ	βασιλεῖς	(do.)
Acc.	βασιλέα	βασιλεῖς	(for βασιλέας)
Gen.	βασιλέως	βασιλέων	
Dat.	βασιλεῖ	βασιλεῦσι	

THE THIRD DECLENSION

Note (1) the ordinary accusative ending -εα, (2) the nom., voc. and acc. plural in -εες and -εας; contract these double vowels to ει (for the sake of sound).

Like βασιλεύς are γραμματεύς, a scribe; γονεύς, a parent.

NEUTER NOUNS OF THE THIRD DECLENSION

These are important, and are of two chief kinds. Remember that all neuters have the same form for the nominative, vocative and accusative cases.

(1) Most conform to the example ῥῆμα on p. 48.

Learn the following :—

αἷμα	blood	ὄνομα	a name
γράμμα	a letter	πνεῦμα	a spirit
θέλημα	a will	στόμα	a mouth
κρίμα	a judgment	σῶμα	a body

There are a few words not ending in -μα which are neuter and come here, such as πῦρ, fire (genitive πυρός); φῶς, light (genitive φωτός); τέρας, a wonder (genitive τέρατος).

(2) Other neuters ending in -ος have some

59

contracted endings. The following model must be memorised :—

γένος, a race, generation

	Singular	Plural
Nom.	γένος	(γένεα) γένη
Voc.	γένος	(γένεα) γένη
Acc.	γένος	(γένεα) γένη
Gen.	(γένεος) γένους	(γενέων) γενῶν
Dat.	γένει	γένεσι

Note I—The genitive singular γένεος contracts to γένους; the nominative, vocative and accusative γένεα contract to γένη ; the genitive plural γενέων to γενῶν.

Note II—These neuters in -ος, must be distinguished from second declension masculine nouns ending in -ος like λόγος (Lesson III). The student will soon become accustomed to the two varieties as found in the New Testament.

Note III—These neuter plurals in -η (for -εα) must be distinguished from first declension feminines ending in -η, like πύλη (Lesson II). The context generally helps to distinguish.

ADJECTIVES CONTAINING THIRD DECLENSION FORMS

These are of two kinds : (1) Those which contain endings of the first declension as well as

THIRD DECLENSION ADJECTIVES

the third. (2) Those which have the same form in the masculine and feminine.

(*I*) These adjectives are of great importance; the verbal adjectives, called participles, are formed on these models. As the participles run parallel to the adjectives now to be learnt we shall take them together.

ADJECTIVES

Form 1 : ἑκών, -οῦσα, -όν, willing

Singular

	Masculine	Feminine	Neuter
Nom.	ἑκών	ἑκοῦσα	ἑκόν
Voc.	ἑκών	ἑκοῦσα	ἑκόν
Acc.	ἑκόντα	ἑκοῦσαν	ἑκόν
Gen.	ἑκόντος	ἑκούσης	ἑκόντος
Dat.	ἑκόντι	ἑκούσῃ	ἑκόντι

Plural

	Masculine	Feminine	Neuter
Nom.	ἑκόντες	ἑκοῦσαι	ἑκόντα
Voc.	ἑκόντες	ἑκοῦσαι	ἑκόντα
Acc.	ἑκόντας	ἑκούσας	ἑκόντα
Gen.	ἑκόντων	ἑκουσῶν	ἑκόντων
Dat.	ἑκοῦσι	ἑκούσαις	ἑκοῦσι

Note—The feminine conforms to the first declension (see γλῶσσα, Lesson III), the masculine and neuter to the third declension.

61

Form II : πᾶς, πᾶσα, πᾶν, all, every

	Singular			Plural		
	M.	F.	N.	M.	F.	N.
Nom.	πᾶς	πᾶσα	πᾶν	πάντες	πᾶσαι	πάντα
Voc.	πᾶς	πᾶσα	πᾶν	πάντες	πᾶσαι	πάντα
Acc.	πάντα	πᾶσαν	πᾶν	πάντας	πάσας	πάντα
Gen.	παντός	πάσης	παντός	πάντων	πασῶν	πάντων
Dat.	παντί	πάσῃ	παντί	πᾶσι	πάσαις	πᾶσι

PARTICIPLES

Present Participles

Present participles of the active voice of the verb are formed exactly like the above. They are verbal adjectives, and qualify nouns just as adjectives do. In Greek the present participle of εἰμί (see Lesson III) is, in its three genders, ὤν, οὖσα, ὄν. Notice that, if we take away the ἐκ- of ἐκών above, we have the participial forms in full. Thus ὤν, "being," is declined as follows :—

	Singular			Plural		
	M.	F.	N.	M.	F.	N.
Nom.	ὤν	οὖσα	ὄν	ὄντες	οὖσαι	ὄντα
Voc.	ὤν	οὖσα	ὄν	ὄντες	οὖσαι	ὄντα
Acc.	ὄντα	οὖσαν	ὄν	ὄντας	οὖσας	ὄντα
Gen.	ὄντος	οὖσης	ὄντος	ὄντων	οὐσῶν	ὄντων
Dat.	ὄντι	οὖσῃ	ὄντι	οὖσι	οὖσαις	οὖσι

PRESENT PARTICIPLES

Coming now again to the verb λύω, the present participle is λύων, λύουσα, λῦον, and signifies "loosing." These various forms may qualify some noun or pronoun or may simply qualify the definite article. In every case there is agreement in case, number and gender. Thus in Heb. 1, 7, ὁ ποιῶν is literally "The (One) making," translated "Who maketh." Again, in 1 Cor. 15, 57, τῷ δὲ Θεῷ χάρις τῷ διδόντι literally is "But to God thanks, the (One) giving" ἡμῖν, to us, τὸ νῖκος, the victory (for νῖκος see γένος, above); in Jas. 1, 5, παρὰ τοῦ διδόντος Θεοῦ is "from the giving God." In the following sentence note the feminine participle λέγουσαν "saying," in agreement with the fem. φωνήν, "a voice": ἤκουσεν (he heard, 1st aorist of ἀκούω, I hear) φωνὴν λέγουσαν αὐτῷ Σαούλ Σαούλ (Saul, Saul), τί (why) με διώκεις; "persecutest thou" (Acts 9, 4).

Exercise

Translate the following (after learning the vocabulary), correcting your result from the English version. Then re-translate into Greek, correcting your result from the Greek text.

Ἴδε	Behold	ἁμαρτάνω	I sin
ἀμνός	a lamb	ἀγάπη	love
αἴρω	I bear, take away	μένω	I abide
ποιέω	I do	μαρτυρία	witness
διάβολος	Devil	μή	not
ἀπ᾽ ἀρχῆς	from (the) beginning	αἰώνιος-ος-ον	eternal
		ἔχω	I have

63

(1) Ἴδε ὁ Ἀμνὸς τοῦ Θεοῦ ὁ αἴρων τὴν ἁμαρτίαν τοῦ κόσμου (John 1, 29)—note the article ὁ and the participle αἴρων agreeing with it ; this is literally " the (One) bearing."

(2) 1 John 3, 8, as far as ἁμαρτάνει.

(3) 1 John 4, 16, from ὁ Θεός to μένει at the end of the sentence.

(4) 1 John 5, 10, first sentence only, ending with αὐτῷ.

(5) 1 John 5, 11-12—note that αἰώνιος has the same form in the feminine as the masculine—hence αἰώνιον is feminine agreeing with ζωήν, though the form looks like a masculine.

ἔδωκεν is " gave " ; its subject is ὁ Θεός.

LESSON X

The Participles of the Active Voice

(Continued)

As the present participle, ending in -ων, -ουσα, -ον (e.g., λύων, " loosing ") corresponds to the present tense, indicative (λύω, " I loose") and is really an adjective (see last Lesson), so *the future participle* (e.g., λύσων, " being about to loose ") corresponds to the future tense, indicative (λύσω, " I will loose"; see the verb λύω, Lesson VI). This future participle is declined in exactly the same way as the present participle in all cases, numbers and genders. Hence this participle of λύω is λύσων, λύσουσα, λῦσον. (Revise the present participle in Lesson IX and form this on the model with the added σ in the middle of the word.) The use of the future participle is rare.

There is no participle corresponding to the imperfect tense indicative (ἔλυον, Lesson VI).

The *first aorist participle* ends in -ας, -ασα, -αν, and is declined exactly like the adjective πᾶς, πᾶσα, πᾶν (see Lesson IX). This participle corresponds to the first aorist indicative (e.g., ἔλυσα, " I loosed," see Lesson VI). Thus the

65

aorist participle of λύω is λύσας, λύσασα, λῦσαν (three genders). Notice that the augment, ἐ- (in ἔλυσα) is dropped; that is to say, the participle is not ἔλυσας but λύσας. There is no augment outside the indicative mood.

The student should write out the singular and plural, in all genders and cases, of λύσας, λύσασα, λῦσαν, from memory, on the model of πᾶς, πᾶσα, πᾶν.

The first aorist participle is very common. Study the following passages :—

(a) ὁ πέμψας με is " The (One) having sent me " : πέμψας is the nom. sing. masc., first aorist participle of πέμπω, " I send " (future πέμψω, " I will send," i.e., for πέμπσω, -πσ becoming ψ): it agrees in case, number and gender with the article ὁ.

(b) ἵνα ("in order that ") ἀπόκρισιν (" an answer "—accusative of ἀπόκρισις) δῶμεν (" we may give ") τοῖς (" to the [ones] ") πέμψασιν (" having sent ") ἡμᾶς (" us "). Note that πέμψασιν is the dative plural masc., in agreement with τοῖς. This use of the participle in agreement with the article is very frequent.

Corresponding to the perfect indicative (e.g.,

ACTIVE VOICE PARTICIPLES

λέλυκα " I have loosed," see Lesson VI) is *the perfect participle*, which ends in -ως, -υια, -ος. Thus, the perfect participle of λύω is λελυκώς, λελυκυῖα, λελυκός (three genders). The accusative is λελυκότα, λελυκυῖαν, λελυκός ; the masculine and neuter have third declension endings, and the feminine has first declension endings, with -α- throughout, because the preceding letter is a vowel, -ι-, and not a consonant (see Lesson III, Note I).

The indicative mood tenses and participles thus far learnt may be set out as follows :—

Indicative Mood (1st Person)		*Participles* (Nominative)		
Present	λύω	λύων,	λύουσα,	λῦον
Imperfect	ἔλυον	none		
Future	λύσω	λύσων,	λύσουσα,	λῦσον
First Aorist	ἔλυσα	λύσας,	λύσασα,	λῦσαν
Perfect	λέλυκα	λελυκώς,	λελυκυῖα,	λελυκός
Pluperfect	ἐλελύκειν	none		

Exercise—The student who has gone carefully through the Lessons up to this point will now be able, with a vocabulary and the translation of a few words here and there (to be explained later), to render considerable portions of the New Testament. We will take the first seven lines of the Epistle to the Hebrews. Learn the meanings given in brackets and refer to the various places in the past Lessons

67

as mentioned. Study the passages again and again. Re-translate it. If time permits learn it by heart.

πολυμερῶς (an adverb meaning "by many portions") καὶ πολυτρόπως ("in many ways") πάλαι ("formerly" or "of old") ὁ Θεὸς λαλήσας (1st aorist participle of λαλέω, I speak—see λύσας above—"having spoken") τοῖς πατράσιν (dative plural of πατήρ—see Lesson VIII) ἐν ("by"— ἐν often has this meaning instead of "in") τοῖς προφήταις (see under μαθητής, Note III, Lesson III), ἐπ' (for ἐπί, a preposition which, when followed by the genitive case, means "at": the ι is omitted before the ἐ- of the next word) ἐσχάτου (ἔσχατος, -η, -ον, "last" "the" is understood: "at the last" or "at the end") τῶν ἡμερῶν τούτων (ἡμέρα, "a day": for τούτων see Lesson IV, and Rule II; note that the order here is the same as in ἡ φωνὴ αὕτη, i.e., article noun, demonstrative adjective) ἐλάλησεν (3rd person singular 1st aorist of λαλέω) ἡμῖν (to us) ἐν Υἱῷ ὃν (Lesson V, here accusative as the object of ἔθηκεν) ἔθηκεν ("He appointed") κληρονόμον ("heir"—accus. sing., agreeing in case and gender with ὅν) πάντων ("of all things"—gen. plur. neut. of πᾶς—lit. "of all") δι' (for διά, which, when followed by the genitive, means "by") οὗ (see Lesson V—genitive case— "whom") καὶ ("also") ἐποίησεν (1st aorist of ποιέω, I make) τοὺς αἰῶνας (Lesson VII) ὃς ὢν (present participle of εἰμί—"being") ἀπαύγασμα (an effulgence, or shining forth—the article " the " is not here expressed in Greek, but must be inserted in English) τῆς δοξης (Lesson III, Note II, and Vocab.—here the article signifies " the glory (of Him)," i.e., " His glory ") καὶ χαρακτὴρ (" impress " or " very image "— our word " character " is a transliteration of it, but not here a translation) τῆς ὑποστάσεως (ὑπόστασις " substance "—like πόλις, Lesson IX) αὐτοῦ (lit. " of Him," i.e., " His "—see αὐτός, Lesson V), φέρων (pres. participle of φέρω, I bear, uphold) τε (" and "—always comes second in the clause) τὰ πάντα (" all things "—acc. plur. neut.—the article τά is not to be translated) τῷ (" by the "—the dative case here expresses the instrument, and is called the instrumental dative ; hence we must translate by " by ") ῥήματι (dative of ῥῆμα, see Lesson VII, page 48) τῆς δυνάμεως (gen. case of δύναμις, power, like πόλις) αὐτοῦ (" His ").

Translate verses 7 and 8 of the same chapter, with the help of the following vocabulary :—

εὐθύτης	uprightness	ῥάβδος	a sceptre
πῦρ	fire	πρός	to
φλόξ	a flame	μέν	indeed
λειτουργός	a minister	λέγω	I say

Note that ὁ ποιῶν is " the (One) making " (present participle—we must render by " who maketh ") : ὁ Θεός is " O God " : the next phrase is literally "unto the age of the age," but its English equivalent is "for ever and ever" and it must be so translated.

Third Declension Adjectives
of Two Terminations

These have no separate form for the feminine. There are two kinds. The first kind consists of a simple form ending in -ων, with stem ending -ον, and therefore with genitive ending in -ονος etc. This must be distinguished from the adjectives ending in -ων (with genitive ending -οντος) which have three forms for the three genders (see ἑκών, ἑκοῦσα, ἑκόν, Lesson IX).

The following is an example :—

σώφρων, sober minded (stem, σωφρον-)

	Singular		Plural	
	M. & F.	Neut.	M. & F.	Neut.
Nom.	σώφρων	σῶφρον	σώφρονες	σώφρονα
Voc.	σῶφρον	σῶφρον	σώφρονες	σώφρονα
Acc.	σώφρονα	σῶφρον	σώφρονας	σώφρονα
Gen.	σώφρονος	σώφρονος	σωφρόνων	σωφρόνων
Dat.	σώφρονι	σώφρονι	σώφροσι	σώφροσι

The second kind ends in -ης (neut. -ες). It contracts double vowels into a single sound. *This is a large and important class of adjective.* The contracted forms in the following paradigm must be memorised thoroughly (the uncontracted forms in brackets are quite regular and the endings will already be known).

ἀληθής, -ές, true

Singular

	Masc. & Fem.		Neut.
Nom.		ἀληθής	ἀληθές
Voc.		ἀληθές	ἀληθές
Acc.	(ἀληθέα)	ἀληθῆ	ἀληθές
Gen.	(ἀληθέος)	ἀληθοῦς	ἀληθοῦς
Dat.	(ἀληθέϊ)	ἀληθεῖ	ἀληθεῖ

Plural

	Masc. & Fem.		Neut.	
N.	(ἀληθέες)	ἀληθεῖς	(ἀληθέα)	ἀληθῆ
V.	(„)	ἀληθεῖς	(„)	ἀληθῆ
A.	(—έας)	ἀληθεῖς	(„)	ἀληθῆ
G.	(—έων)	ἀληθῶν	(—έων)	ἀληθῶν
D.		ἀληθέσι		ἀληθέσι

F

LESSON XI

PERSONAL PRONOUNS

Commit the following to memory :—

First Person

	Singular			Plural	
Nom.	ἐγώ		I	ἡμεῖς	we
Acc.	ἐμέ or	με	me	ἡμᾶς	us
Gen.	ἐμοῦ or	μου	of me	ἡμῶν	of us
Dat.	ἐμοί or	μοι	to me	ἡμῖν	to us

Second Person

	Singular		Plural	
Nom.	σύ	thou	ὑμεῖς	you or ye
Acc.	σέ	thee	ὑμᾶς	you
Gen.	σοῦ	of thee	ὑμῶν	of you
Dat.	σοί	to thee	ὑμῖν	to you

For the *Third Person*, " he, she, it," αὐτός, αὐτή, αὐτό, see Lesson V.

REFLEXIVE PRONOUNS

In English these end in " -self," " -selves." They are used when the object of a sentence or clause refers to the same person or thing as the subject.

Forms occurring in the New Testament are the following :—

ἐμαυτόν	myself	ἑαυτό (αὐτό)	itself
σεαυτόν	thyself	ἑαυτούς	ourselves, or
ἑαυτόν (or αὐτόν)			yourselves, or
	himself		themselves

72

PRONOUNS

ἑαυτήν (or αὐτήν)   ἑαυτῶν of yourselves
        herself   ἑαυτοῖς to yourselves
ἑαυτοῦ   of thyself

Note I—When αὐτός, -ή, -ό immediately follows a noun or pronoun with which it is connected it means " self." Thus ὁ ἄνθρωπος αὐτός is " the man himself " ; ὁ αὐτὸς ἄνθρωπος is " the same man."

Note II—This use of αὐτός as a reflexive must carefully be distinguished from the personal use " he." When used in the nominative for the third person, it is always emphatic : e.g., αὐτὸς ἐγὼ . . . δουλεύω, I myself serve (Rom. 7, 25) : αὐτοὶ γὰρ ὑμεῖς θεοδίδακτοί ἐστε, for ye yourselves are taught of God (lit. God-taught) (1 Thess. 4, 9).

Note III—The ε- of ἑαυτόν, etc., is often dropped and the word contracted to αὐτόν, etc. In that case αὐτός, " himself," and the other forms must be distinguished from αὐτός, " he," etc.

Note IV—This third person reflexive pronoun is also used for the first and second persons, when there would be no ambiguity. Thus ἐν ἑαυτοῖς is " in ourselves," (Rom. 8, 23) instead of ἐν ἡμῖν αὐτοῖς. Again, τὴν ἑαυτῶν σωτηρίαν is " your own salvation," lit., " the salvation of yourselves " (Phil. 2, 12) instead of τὴν ὑμῶν αὐτῶν σωτηρίαν.

Other examples are : βλέπετε δὲ ὑμεῖς ἑαυτούς, " But take ye heed to yourselves " (Mark 13, 9 ; cp. 2 John 8) ; προσέχετε ἑαυτοῖς " take heed to yourselves " (Luke 12, 1).

73

*(Revise the demonstrative pronouns, **Lesson IV**, and the personal and relative pronouns, **Lesson V**)*

INDEFINITE PRONOUNS

The pronoun τις (masc. and fem.), τι (neut.) means " someone," " anyone," " a certain," " some," " any." It is declined as follows, the masculine and feminine being the same, and the endings those of the third declension :—

	Singular		Plural	
	M. & F.	Neut.	M. & F.	Neut.
Nom.	τις	τι	τινες	τινα
Acc.	τινα	τι	τινας	τινα
Gen.	τινος	τινος	τινων	τινων
Dat.	τινι	τινι	τισι	τισι

Examples—εἰσίν τινες ὧδε, there are some here (Mark 9, 1) ; Ἑκατοντάρχου δέ τινος (and of a certain centurion) δοῦλος (a servant), (Luke 7, 2) ; Ἄνθρωπός τις ἦν πλούσιος, " (there) was a certain rich man," lit., " a certain man was rich " (Luke 16, 1) ; οὔτε (nor) ὕψωμα (height) οὔτε (nor) βάθος (depth) οὔτε (nor) τις (any) κτίσις (creature) ἑτέρα (other) (Rom. 8, 39).

Note I—The indefinite pronoun τις never stands first in a sentence.

Note II—If used with a noun it generally follows the noun.

Note III—Other indefinite pronouns are οὔτις and μήτις, each of which means "no one." They

are formed by the addition of τις to the negatives
οὐ and μή, "not."

INTERROGATIVE PRONOUNS

The simple interrogative pronoun is τίς, τί,
who ? what ? In form it is exactly like the
indefinite pronoun τις, τι, the only difference being
that it has an accent pointing from left to right.
The two must be carefully distinguished.

Examples—Τίς ἐστιν ἡ μήτηρ μου, καὶ τίνες εἰσὶν
οἱ ἀδελφοί μου, Who is My mother, and who are
My brethren? (Matt. 12, 48); τίνα σεαυτὸν ποιεῖς;
Whom makest Thou Thyself ? (John 8, 53).

There is an adjectival use of τίς, in agreement
with a noun, e.g., Τί σημεῖον (What sign) δεικνύεις
(showest Thou) ἡμῖν (to us) ; (John 2, 18).

The following interrogative pronouns should
also be memorised ; they correspond to the
relative pronouns οἷος and ὅσος given below.
They are all of 1st and 2nd declension endings.

Qualitative, ποῖος, -α, -ον, of what kind ?
Quantitative, πόσος, -η, -ον, how great ?

The plural πόσοι, -αι, -α signifies " how
many ? "

There is a relative pronoun, ὁποῖος, " of what
kind," corresponding to ποῖος, and occurring five
times in the New Testament. In Acts 26, 29, it is
rendered " such as " ; in 1 Cor. 3, 13 " of what
sort"; in Gal. 2, 6 " whatsoever "; in 1 Thess.
1, 9 and Jas. 1, 24 " what manner of."

75

An indefinite relative, " whoever," " whatever," is formed by combining τις, τι, with ὅς, ἥ, ὅ, both parts being declined as follows :—

Singular

	Masc.	Fem.	Neut.
Nom.	ὅστις	ἥτις	ὅ,τι
Acc.	ὅντινα	ἥντινα	ὅ,τι
Gen.	οὗτινος	ἧστινος	οὗτινος
Dat.	ᾧτινι	ᾗτινι	ᾧτινι

Plural

	Masc.	Fem.	Neut.
N.	οἵτινες	αἵτινες	ἅτινα
A.	οὕστινας	ἅστινας	ἅτινα
G.	ὧντινων	ὧντινων	ὧντινων
D.	οἷστισι	αἷστισι	οἷστισι

Note—The genitive singular masculine is shortened to ὅτου in the phrase ἕως ὅτου " as long as," " until," lit., "until whatever (time)." (See Matt. 5, 25).

Other relative pronouns are as follows :—

Qualitative, οἷος -α, -ον, such as.
Quantitative, ὅσος, -η, -ον, so great as,
and its plural ὅσοι, -αι, α, so many as.
Compare the interrogatives above, ποῖος and πόσος.

The following table will sum up the chief pronouns which correspond to one another :—

Demonstrative	Relative	Interrogative	Indefinite
οὗτος (this)	ὅς (who)	τίς (who ?)	τις (someone)
τοιοῦτος (such an one)	οἷος (such as)	ποῖος (of what sort ?)	—
τοσοῦτος (so great)	ὅσος (so great as)	πόσος (how great ?)	—
τοσοῦτοι (so many)	ὅσοι (so many as)	πόσοι (how many ?)	—

DISTRIBUTIVE PRONOUNS

(1) ἄλλος, ἄλλη, ἄλλο, another (i.e., another of the same sort, of like kind). The plural of this denotes "others." It is declined like ὅς, ἥ, ὅ.

(2) ἕτερος, ἑτέρα, ἕτερον, another (i.e., another of a different kind).

(3) ἀλλήλους, ἀλλήλων, ἀλλήλοις, each other, of each other, to each other ; this is used only in the accusative, genitive and dative plural.

(4) ἕκαστος, -η, -ον, each ; this is used only in the singular.

Vocabulary and Exercise

Learn the following words and translate the passages below, correcting your rendering from the English Revised Version ; re-translate the English into the Greek without referring to the exercise, and correct your Greek from the exercise.

οἰκοδομέω	I build	μέν	indeed
οἰκία	a house	δέ	but
πέτρα	a rock	κύριος	lord
πρός	to (followed by the accusative)	φυτεύω	I plant
		ποτίζω	I water
		οὖν	therefore
ἀληθινός	true	διάκονος	a minister
σπείρω	I sow	ὡς	as
θερίζω	I reap	ὥστε	so then, or
ποῦ	where ?		so that

PRONOUNS

γογγυσμός	a mur- muring	ποιέω	I do
περί	concerning	ἀκούω	I hear
ὄχλος	a multitude	οὔτε	neither, nor
		φρόνιμος	prudent

Translate with the help of the accompanying notes :—

I—1 Cor. 3, 4-7, beginning with Ἐγὼ μέν εἰμι . . . Note the special significance of ἕτερος, "another" of a different character, not another of the same sort (ἄλλος) : δι' is for διά, which with the genitive (ὧν) denotes "by means of" : ἐπιστεύσατε, 2nd pers. plural, 1st aor. of πιστεύω : ἔδωκεν "gave" (to be explained later) : note that τί is "what" (neut. of τίς—so in R.V., not "who" as in A.V.), but τι, without the accent in verse 7, is "anything." What is the ἐ- in ἐφύτευσα, and in ἐπότισεν [see Lesson VI, Note III] ? Verbs like ποτίζω ending in -ίζω in the present tense change the ζ to σ in the 1st aorist : ηὔξανεν is the imperfect tense of αὐξάνω "was giving the increase"—note that ἀ- makes the augment ἠ- not ἐα- : ἕν is "one," it is the neuter of εἷς, μία, ἕν (masc., fem., neut.) and is to be distinguished from ἐν, "in." It might be rendered "one thing." Note the four occurrences of the article ὁ with the present participle, (lit., "the one planting," etc.), this must be rendered by "he that planteth," etc.

II—Matt. 7, 24, πᾶς is "every one" ; for μου

see beginning of this Lesson. For τούτους see Lesson IV, Rule II, ὁμοιωθήσεται "shall be likened." ᾠκοδόμησεν is the 3rd pers. sing. of the 1st aorist of οἰκοδομέω; note that the augment of verbs beginning in οἰ is formed by turning the οἰ- into ᾠ with the iota underneath. The future of verbs ending in -έω ends in -ήσω, and the 1st aorist in -ησα.

III—Acts 11, 20. Translate Ἦσαν "there were"; ἐξ is for ἐκ "of" or "out of"; Κύπριοι Cyprians; ἐλθόντες "having come" (see later); ἐλάλουν is the 3rd pers. plur. imperf. tense of λαλέω, "I speak"—the -ουν is for -εον; εὐαγγελιζόμενοι "preaching" (see later).

IV—John 4, 37, ἄλλος . . . ἄλλος is "one . . . another."

V—John 7, 12, οἱ μέν is "some indeed"—the "indeed" should be omitted in translating; οὐ is "No"; πλανᾷ "He deceiveth."

LESSON XII

The Verb (*Continued*)

THE IMPERATIVE MOOD

Having learnt the Indicative Mood (which makes assertions) and the Participles (or Verbal Adjectives), which correspond to the tenses of the Indicative, we have now to consider the Imperative Mood (which makes commands).

There are only three tenses, the Present, which gives a command indicating continuous action, or repeated action (e.g., λῦε. " loose thou, and continue to do so "), the First Aorist, which gives a command without reference to its continuance or frequency (e.g., λῦσον, " loose thou "—a single act) and the Perfect, λέλυκε, " do thou have had loosed, and let it remain so " ; this last is rarely used.

There is no Future Imperative. There are two persons, the second and the third.

The following specimen should be committed to memory and then should be written out in a column parallel to the tenses of the Indicative Mood, tense against tense where they correspond.

81

Present Tense (continuous action)

Singular
2nd pers. λῦε, loose thou
3rd pers. λυέτω, let him loosen

Plural
2nd pers. λύετε, loose ye
3rd pers. λυέτωσαν or
λυόντων, let them loosen

First Aorist (momentary action)

Singular
2nd pers. λῦσον, loose thou
3rd pers. λυσάτω, let him loosen

Plural
2nd pers. λύσατε, loose ye
3rd pers. λυσάτωσαν or
λυσάντων, let them loosen

Perfect

	Singular	Plural
2nd pers.	λέλυκε	λελύκετε
3rd pers.	λελυκέτω	λελυκέτωσαν or
		λελυκόντων

(the meanings are " do thou have had loosed,"
" let him have had loosed," " do ye have had
loosed," " let them have had loosed.")

Note I—There is no augment (ἐ-) in the
1st Aorist of the Imperative, nor indeed does
the augment occur outside the Indicative Mood.

IMPERATIVE MOOD ACTIVE

Note II—Observe the characteristic -σ- of the 1st Aorist, and the characteristic reduplication λε- of the Perfect, as in the Indicative Mood.

Note III—The Aorist Imperative is very frequent in the New Testament and must be carefully noted.

The following vocabulary will be a guide to the exercise below. The student should learn the list, if time permits, at all events the verbs. Then translate the six passages given in the exercise, correcting the result from the English version. Re-translate from the English into Greek, correcting from the Greek version.

ναός	a temple	ἕως	up to
ἀπολύω	I let go	ἄνω	the brim
ἐκεῖνος (see Lesson IV plural " these ")		ἀντλέω	I draw out, (used of water etc.—future ἀντλήσω)
		φέρω	I bear
ὅθεν	wherefore	ἀρχιτρίκλινος	a governor of a feast
ἅγιος, -α, -ον	holy		
κλῆσις	a calling (gen. κλήσεως)	μή	not (always used instead of οὐ with the Imperative)
ἐπουράνιος, -α, -ον	heavenly		
μέτοχος	a partaker	θησαυρίζω	I lay up treasure
κατανοέω	I consider		
Ἀρχιερεύς	High Priest (see Lesson IX)	θησαυρός	a treasure

πιστός, -ή, όν· faithful
ὅλος, -η, -ον all
οἶκος a house

———

γεμίζω I fill (the future is γεμίσω)
ὑδρία a water pot
ὕδωρ water (gen. ὕδατος—to be explained later)

ἐπί upon (when used with a genitive)
γῆ earth
ὅπου where
σής a moth
βρῶσις rust
ἀφανίζω I corrupt
κλέπτης a thief
διορύσσω I break through
κλέπτω I steal
καρδία a heart

Exercise on the Imperative Mood

Translate :—

(1) λύσατε (λύω here means " to destroy ") τὸν ναὸν τοῦτον (John 2, 19). Note the 1st Aorist, 2nd person plur., " destroy ye."

(2) Ἀπόλυσον τοὺς ἀνθρώπους ἐκείνους (Acts 16, 35).

(3) Ὑμεῖς (ye) οὖν (therefore) ἀκούσατε τὴν παραβολήν (Matt. 13, 18—the Ὑμεῖς is emphatic).

(4) Heb. 3, verses 1 and 2, with the aid of the vocab. *Note I*—κατανοήσατε is the 1st Aorist Imperative, 2nd person plural of κατανοέω—verbs ending in -έω make the future end in -ήσω, lengthening the ε to η and so in the 1st Aorist : so ποιέω makes the future ποιήσω : *II*—ὄντα is accus. sing. masc. pres.

participle of εἰμί: *III*—ποιήσαντι is dat. sing. 1st Aorist Participle of ποιέω, I make.

(5) John 2, 7, as far as ἀρχιτρικλίνῳ. The genitive ὕδατος here signifies " with water " (the genitive must be rendered " with," after a verb denoting " to fill "). Note carefully the difference in the tenses of the Imperative Mood verbs in this verse : Γεμίσατε and ἀντλήσατε are 1st aorists " fill ye up," " draw out," a single act in each instance ; but φέρετε is a present tense, " be carrying " (there is, in this change of tense, a peculiarly delicate suggestion of politeness with regard to the recognition of the place of honour held by the governor of the feast).

(6) Matt. 6, 19-21. *Note I*—ὑμῖν (dative plural) " for yourselves," lit., " for you " ; the dative signifies " for " as well as " to," and the personal pronoun here stands for the reflexive pronoun, which in full would be ὑμῖν αὐτοῖς (see Lesson XI, Note IV) : *II*—ἀφανίζει is singular number " doth corrupt," although it has two subjects " moth and rust," the two being regarded as one subject : *III*—for κλέπται compare μαθητής (Lesson III) : *IV*—σου (verse 21) is lit. " of thee," i.e., " thy " : *V*—ἔσται is " shall be," this will be learnt later.

THE SUBJUNCTIVE MOOD

In English the Subjunctive Mood expresses supposition, doubt or uncertainty, and follows the conjunctions if, lest, though, etc. In Greek the scope of the Subjunctive is much wider.

There is no future or imperfect tense and no perfect in the Active Voice save in one irregular verb. Accordingly the following are the only two Subjunctive tenses in the verb λύω and similar verbs. Note the *iota subscript* (i.e., written under) in the 2nd and 3rd persons singular, and the long vowels η or ω in all the persons.

Present Subjunctive

λύω	I may loose	λύωμεν	we may loose
λύῃς	thou mayest loose	λύητε	ye may loose
λύῃ	he may loose	λύωσι	they may loose

First Aorist Subjunctive

The meaning is either " I may loose " or " I may have loosed," etc.

λύσω	λύσωμεν
λύσῃς	λύσητε
λύσῃ	λύσωσι

Note I—The endings are the same in each tense, save for the characteristic σ in the First Aorist.

Note II—There is a Second Aorist in some verbs, with the same meaning as the First. This will be noticed later.

SUBJUNCTIVE MOOD ACTIVE

First Aorist Participles in the Active Voice have terminations corresponding to these. See the paragraphs dealing with the Aorist Participle in Lesson X.

LESSON XIII

The Subjunctive Mood (*Continued*)

The following is the present tense of the Subjunctive Mood of εἰμί, the verb " to be," of which it is the only Subjunctive tense. The student will observe that the words are precisely the same as the endings of the present Subjunctive of λύω (Lesson XII).

Singular		Plural	
ὦ,	I may be	ὦμεν,	we may be
ᾖς,	thou mayst be	ἦτε,	you may be
ᾖ,	he may be	ὦσι(ν),	they may be

The following are the principal uses of the Subjunctive Mood in the New Testament :—

I—It is used in *clauses expressing purpose*. These are known as *Final Clauses* (i.e., as having an end or object in view). They are introduced by such conjunctions as ἵνα and ὅπως, each of which means " in order that," or simply " that," and negatively by ἵνα μή or ὅπως μή, " in order that not " or " lest," or even by μή alone, which when so used means the same thing.

Examples

The following sentences give examples of purpose expressed positively :—

SUBJUNCTIVE MOOD SYNTAX

John 10, 10, 'Εγὼ (I) ἦλθον (came) ἵνα (in order that) ζωὴν (life—the accusative of the object of the verb following) ἔχωσιν (they may have—3rd person plural, pres. subjunctive of ἔχω, I have) καὶ (and) περισσὸν (abundance) ἔχωσιν (they may have) : Matt. 6, 4, ὅπως (in order that) ᾖ (may be) σου ἡ ἐλεημοσύνη (thine alms—lit., of thee the alms) ἐν τῷ κρυπτῷ (in secret—τῷ not to be translated). In the following sentence note that the tenses are 1st Aorist Subjunctive : John 1, 7, οὗτος (This one, i.e., He) ἦλθεν (came) εἰς (for or unto) μαρτυρίαν (a witness), ἵνα (that) μαρτυρήσῃ (he might bear witness—3rd pers. sing. 1st aor. subjunc. of μαρτυρέω, I bear, witness—the future is μαρτυρήσω, I shall bear witness, the -ε- of the present ending being lengthened to -η-) περὶ (concerning) τοῦ φωτός (the light— genitive of φῶς—the preposition περί takes the genitive), ἵνα (that) πάντες (all) πιστεύσωσιν (might believe—3rd pers. plur., 1st aor. subjunc.) δι' (by means of—short for διά, is followed by the genitive) αὐτοῦ (him).

Translate the 8th verse and note the emphatic ἐκεῖνος, " he " (" that one ").

The question arises : What is the difference in meaning between the present subjunctive and the 1st aorist, seeing that both are rendered by " may, etc." ? The answer is that the present signifies continuous or repeated action (as, for example, ἔχωσιν in John 10, 10 above) ; the aorist signifies either single action or action undefined in point of time. Thus in the last instance μαρτυρήσῃ speaks

89

of John's witness without reference to its continuity, and πιστεύσωσιν points to the single act of faith in believing.

Exercise

Translate, with the help of the accompanying notes, 1 Cor. 1, 10 :—

παρακαλῶ, " I exhort " : διά, " by " : ὀνόματος (genitive of ὄνομα, a name—genitive after διά) : τὸ αὐτό, "the same [thing]" (see Lesson V)—this is the accusative, as object of λέγητε (pres. subjunctive of λέγω, "I speak," subjunctive after ἵνα) : μὴ ᾖ, "[there] may not be "—note the negative μή (not οὐ) with the subjunctive : ἐν, "among" (takes the dative) : σχίσματα, "schisms " (note that in Greek a neuter plural subject of a verb takes the verb in the singular ; thus σχίσματα is the subject of ᾖ [singular] " schisms may not be ") : ἦτε (subjunc. of εἰμί—see above) : κατηρτισμένοι, "joined" (explained later) : νοΐ, dative of νοῦς, "mind" (see Lesson VII) : γνώμῃ, " judgment."

(After becoming thoroughly familiarised with this verse, re-translate it, correcting your result.)

II—The subjunctive is used in certain *Conditional Clauses* (these are introduced in English by " if "), which imply either possibility or uncertainty with the prospect of decision. In these cases ἐάν (" if ") is used to introduce the subjunctive. Where the supposition assumes a fact, εἰ (which also means " if ") is used followed by the *indicative*. See also p. 212.

Examples

Thus in Matt. 4, 3, εἰ υἱὸς εἶ τοῦ Θεοῦ, " if Thou art (the) Son of God," does not express uncertainty or possibility, but signifies " assuming that Thou art the Son of God " (εἶ, " thou art," is the 2nd pers. sing. of the pres. indic. of εἰμί—see Lesson III). But in Matt. 17, 20, ἐὰν ἔχητε πίστιν ὡς κόκκον σινάπεως, " if ye have faith as a grain of mustard seed " (ἔχητε being the pres. *subjunctive* of ἔχω, I have) does not assume that they have faith, but suggests an uncertainty with the prospect of fulfilment, hence the subjunctive is used.

Note : ἐάν is really εἰ ἄν and the ἄν determines the use of the subjunctive.

Exercise

Translate with the help of notes and, after thoroughly learning the texts, re-translate from the English into Greek.

(1) John 6, 62 : the " what then " is not expressed in Greek, it is understood ; the Greek sentence simply begins with " if " : θεωρῆτε is pres. subjunc. of θεωρέω, I behold ; ἀναβαίνοντα is acc. sing. masc. of pres. participle of ἀναβαίνω, I ascend ; τὸ πρότερον, lit. " the former," is an adverbial phrase meaning " before."

(2) John 15, 10 : ἐντολάς is acc. plur. of ἐντολή, a commandment, and is the object of the verb τηρήσητε, which is the 1st aor. subj. of τηρέω, I keep: μενεῖτε is the future indic. 2nd pers. plur. of μένω, I abide, and will be explained later. Note the reduplication in τετήρηκα (what tense is this ? See λέλυκα, Lesson VI).

(3) Rom. 2, 25 : περιτομή, circumcision : μέν, indeed : ὠφελεῖ, " profiteth "—3rd pers. sing. pres. indic. of ὠφελέω, I profit : νόμον, " the Law "—the object of πράσσης, " thou doest " (pres. subjunc. of πράσσω : δέ, but : παραβάτης, a transgressor : ἧς, " thou art "—pres. subjunc. of εἰμί (see above) : ἀκροβυστία, uncircumcision : γέγονεν, " has become " (to be explained later).

III—The subjunctive is used in *clauses beginning with a relative pronoun or adverb*, like " whoever," " whenever," or " wherever," *which do not refer to a definite person or thing ;* in other words, when the word " ever " can be used after the relative.

Note that ἄν or ἐάν follows the relative. This ἄν is not translateable, it simply has a generalising effect in these clauses. The ἄν is joined to ὅτε, " when," making ὅταν " whenever." Two other relatives to be memorised are ὅπου, " where," and ἕως, " until."

Examples

(1) Matt. 18, 6 : ὃς δ᾽ ἄν (" but whosoever "—the

92

relative pronoun ὅς with ἄν makes "whosoever":
δ' is for δέ, "but"; it never comes first in the
sentence) σκανδαλίσῃ (shall cause to stumble—3rd
pers. sing. 1st aorist, subjunc. of σκανδαλίζω—ζ in
the present tense becomes σ in the future and 1st
aorist) ἕνα ("one"—accus. masc. of εἷς—the
numerals will be given later) τῶν μικρῶν τούτων (of
these little [ones]) τῶν πιστευόντων (the [ones]
believing) εἰς ἐμέ (on Me).

(2) John 2, 5: ὅ τι ἄν (ὅστις is "whosoever"
and the neuter ὅτι is written separately, ὅ τι, or
with a comma between, ὅ, τι) λέγῃ (He saith—
pres. subjunc.) ὑμῖν (to you) ποιήσατε (do ye—2nd
pers. plur. 1st aorist imperative of ποιέω).

(3) Matt. 6, 2: ὅταν (whensoever—a relative
adverb, for ὅτε ἄν) οὖν (therefore) ποιῇς (thou doest
—pres. subjunc.) ἐλεημοσύνην (alms), μὴ σαλπίσῃς
(do not sound a trumpet—1st aor. subjunc. of
σαλπίζω—μή with the 1st aor. subjunc. stands for
the imperative) ἔμπροσθέν (before—takes the genitive) σου (thee).

Translate John 9, 5: ὅταν, "when" (see R.V.):
ὦ, "I am" (pres. subjunc. of εἰμί, see above).

IV—The Subjunctive is used in *Deliberative
Questions*, i.e., when persons are deliberating as to
what is to be done. This is known as the Deliberate
Subjunctive. Thus, "Shall we continue in sin?"
is ἐπιμένωμεν τῇ ἁμαρτίᾳ; (Rom. 6, 1): ἐπιμένωμεν
(note the long ω) is 1st pers. plur. pres. subjunc. of

ἐπιμένω, a compound of ἐπί and μένω, " I abide " ;
the article τῇ is not to be translated, as it is used
with abstract nouns such as ἁμαρτία, i.e., when it
denotes sin in general. The dative case must here
be translated " in sin." The dative case has several
significances, which must be rendered appropriately
in English according to the word which governs the
noun. This will be explained later.

V—The Subjunctive is used in *certain forms of
exhortation.* This is called *The Hortatory Subjunctive.* In English it is introduced by " let." Thus
1 Thess. 5, 6, γρηγορῶμεν καὶ νήφωμεν is " let us
watch and let us be sober " ; note the long ω in
distinction from the pres. Indicative ; the first
verb is the present subjunctive, first person plural
of γρηγορέω, " I watch," and the second verb is
the same tense and person of νήφω, " I am sober."

*The student should become thoroughly familiar with
the whole of this lesson before taking up the next. The
use of the Subjunctive is very important. The
examples given should be read again and again until
the student can easily re-translate them from English
into Greek. For further treatment of the Subjunctive
see the additional rules of Syntax.*

LESSON XIV

Extra Note on Negative Commands or Prohibitions

For these the Imperative Mood is used, or in certain instances the Subjunctive. The student should revise the Imperative Mood of λύω (Lesson XII) and learn now the Imperative of εἰμί, which is as follows :—

ἴσθι, be thou	ἔστε, be ye
ἔστω or ἤτω, let him (or her, or it) be, or let there be.	ἔστωσαν, let them be

Note : The negative in prohibitions is always μή.

I—The *Present Imperative* with μή most frequently denotes a command to cease to do something, or not to do what is already being done. Thus μὴ κλαίετε is " do not weep," and in Matt. 6, 19, μὴ θησαυρίζετε is "do not treasure" ὑμῖν (for yourselves) θησαυροὺς ἐπὶ τῆς γῆς (on the earth).

II—When a command is given not to do something at all, not to begin to do something, μή with the *Aorist Subjunctive* is used. As an example study again the sentence in *III*, (3), Lesson XIII from Matt. 6, 2, noticing the latter part of the verse :—ὅταν οὖν ποιῇς ἐλεημοσύνην μὴ σαλπίσῃς (do not sound a trumpet—σαλπίσῃς is the 2nd pers. sing. 1st Aorist Subjunctive). Here the command is not to begin that practice.

Exercise

(1) The student should now be able to translate the whole of Matt. 6, 19-23. Some of this has already been given. Write out a translation with the help of the following vocabulary. If any noun is forgotten, turn to the English Version (preferably the R.V.), but try to translate without doing this. Re-translate the passage into Greek.

ἀφανίζω	I consume	σῶμα	body
διορύσσω	I dig through	ὀφθαλμός	eye
κλέπτω	I steal	ἁπλοῦς	single
ἐκεῖ	there	ὅλος-η-ον	all or (the) whole
ἔσται	3rd sing. fut. of εἰμί	φωτεινός-ή-όν	full of light
καί	also (verse 21)	πονηρός	evil
καρδία	heart	σκοτεινός	full of darkness
λύχνος	lamp	πόσος	how great

(2) ἡ πίστις (faith) σου (of thee—i.e., " thy faith ") σέσωκέ (perf. of σώζω, I save) σε · ὕπαγε (go) εἰς εἰρήνην (peace) καὶ ἴσθι (see Imperative of εἰμί above) ὑγιὴς (whole) ἀπὸ (from, with genitive) τῆς μάστιγός σου (μάστιξ, a scourge, plague—genitive μάστιγος), Mark 5, 34.

(3) ἔστω (let be) δὲ ὁ λόγος (speech) ὑμῶν ναὶ (yea) ναί, οὔ οὔ. For ἔστω see Imperative of εἰμί, above, Matt. 5, 36.

(4) Jas. 5, 12 (middle of verse)—μὴ ὀμνύετε (ὀμνύω, I swear) . . . ἤτω (" let be "—see the Imperative of εἰμί) δὲ ὑμῶν τό Ναὶ (lit., " the nay of you ") ναί, καὶ τὸ Οὔ οὔ.

THE OPTATIVE MOOD

This Mood is used either (a) in expressing wishes or (b) in what are called dependent questions, or (c) in deliberative questions. Further details are given later. The use of the Optative is not frequent in New Testament.

Memorise the following :—

The Optative Mood of εἰμί
" I might be," etc.

Singular	Plural		
εἴην	εἴημεν	or	εἶμεν
εἴης	εἴητε	or	εἶτε
εἴη	εἴησαν	or	εἶεν

The Optative Mood of λύω.

Present
(The precise meaning is determined by the context.)
" I might loose," etc.

Singular	Plural
λύοιμι	λύοιμεν
λύοις	λύοιτε
λύοι	λύοιεν

Future

" I should loose," etc.

Singular	Plural
λύσοιμι	λύσοιμεν
λύσοις	λύσοιτε
λύσοι	λύσοιεν

First Aorist

" I might loose," etc. (according to context)

Singular	Plural
λύσαιμι	λύσαιμεν
λύσαις	λύσαιτε
λύσαι or	λύσαιεν or
λύσειε	λύσειαν

EXAMPLES OF THE OPTATIVE MOOD

(*a*) The following are examples of the expression of a wish :—

(1) τὸ ἀργύριόν σου σὺν σοὶ εἴη εἰς ἀπώλειαν (Acts 8, 20). This is literally " Thy money with thee be unto destruction " (εἴη, 3rd sing. opt. of εἰμί, here simply means " be," i.e., " may [it] be ").

(2) 1 Thess. 3, 12 : ὑμᾶς (" you "—the accus. object of the two succeeding verbs) δὲ ὁ κύριος (the Lord) πλεονάσαι (make to increase—3rd sing. 1st aor. opt. of πλεονάζω, i.e., may He make to increase) καὶ περισσεύσαι (make to abound—same tense of περισσεύω) τῇ ἀγάπῃ (in love—dative of the point in which the verb is applied : hence we must translate by " in " though there is no preposition in the Greek : the article is used because the

OPTATIVE MOOD ACTIVE

noun is abstract) εἰς ἀλλήλους (to one another).

(b) The following are examples of dependent questions, i.e., questions which are not asked directly, but depend upon some preceding statement :—

(1) Ὡς (as, or while) δὲ ἐν ἑαυτῷ (in himself) διηπόρει (was doubting—3rd pers. sing. imperf. indic. of διαπορέω—for διηπόρεε, the -εε contracting to -ει—the change from α to η is due to the fact that when a preposition, here διά, is joined to a verb, here ἀπορέω, the augment, which must come before the verb, joins with the vowel of the preposition, α and η combining to form η thus, not διαηπόρει but διηπόρει) ὁ Πέτρος (Peter—the article is used with proper names) τί (what) ἂν εἴη (might be—the ἂν is not translated) τὸ ὅραμα (the vision). Note that εἴη is in the optative as the question is not asked directly " What is the vision ? " but indirectly, depending on the statement " Peter doubted in himself " (Acts 10, 17).

(2) ἀνακρίνοντες (searching—pres. participle, nom. plur. of ἀνακρίνω, I search) τὰς γραφὰς (the Scriptures) εἰ ἔχοι ταῦτα οὕτως (literally, if these [things] had thus—ταῦτα is the neuter plur. " these [things] " and is the subject of ἔχοι—*neuter plurals take the verb in the singular*—ἔχοι is the optative of ἔχω, I have, and the optative is used because instead of the direct question "Are these things so ? " it is put in an indirect way, " searching if

99

these things were so." The use of ἔχω is idiomatic. That is, whereas the Greek is " if these things had so," we must say " if these things were so " (Acts 17, 11).

(c) The following is an example of a deliberative question, i.e., a direct question asked not simply for the sake of information but in a rhetorical way :—

καί τινες ἔλεγον (and some were saying) Τί ἂν θέλοι (What would—optative of θέλω, I will, I wish) ὁ σπερμολόγος οὗτος (this babbler) λέγειν (say—infinitive mood, see below), Acts 17, 18.

Exercise

Translate, with the help of the accompanying notes :—

1) 2 Thess. 3, 5 : κατευθύναι is the 1st aorist, optative of κατευθύνω, I direct (the omission of the -σ-, which marks the future and 1st aorist tenses, will be explained later) : καρδία, heart : ὑπομονή, patience (note " the patience of Christ "—not as in the A.V.).

(2) Luke 8, 9 : Ἐπηρώτων is " were asking " (for this form see later) : μαθητής, a disciple : τίς, " what " (feminine, agreeing with παραβολή, a parable), this is the subject of εἴη (optative, " might be ").

(3) Acts 17, 27 from ζητεῖν to αὐτόν : ζητεῖν, to seek (infin.—translated in our Version " that-they-should-seek ") : ἄρα γε, to be translated together " haply " : ψηλαφήσειαν is 3rd pers. plur. 1st aor. optative of ψηλαφάω, I feel after.

LESSON XV

THE INFINITIVE MOOD

The Infinitive (in English expressed by " to," e.g., " to be," " to loose ") is a verbal noun, that is to say, it partakes of the nature both of a verb and a noun.

It has no different forms for cases and persons and is therefore indeclinable.

It is always neuter, and as a noun it may be used with different cases of the neuter article.

As a noun it may stand as the subject or as the object of another verb or be governed by a preposition.

As a verb it may itself have a subject or an object. All these points are illustrated below.

Memorise the following :.

Infinitive Mood of εἰμί.

Present Infin.	εἶναι,	to be.
Future ,,	ἔσεσθαι,	to be about to be.

Infinitive Mood, Active, of λύω

Present Infin.	λύειν,	to loose.
Future ,,	λύσειν,	to be about to loose.
1st Aor. ,,	λῦσαι,	to loose at once.
Perfect ,,	λελυκέναι,	to have loosed.

SOME EXAMPLES OF THE INFINITIVE MOOD

(1) Where the Infinitive, as a noun, is the subject of another verb :

καλὸν ἀνθρώπῳ τὸ οὕτως εἶναι, "(it is) good for a man thus to be " (1 Cor. 7, 26). In this sentence the verb ἐστί, " it is," is understood ; i.e., καλόν ἐστι " it is good." Now the subject of this is τὸ οὕτως εἶναι, lit., " the thus to be," i.e., " the thus to be is good " : ἀνθρώπῳ is " for a man."

The article may be omitted : e.g., αἰσχρὸν γάρ ἐστιν (for it is shameful) γυναικὶ (for a woman) λαλεῖν (to speak) ἐν ἐκκλησίᾳ (in church), 1 Cor. 14, 35.

Rule—In such instances, when the Infinitive has a subject, the subject, if expressed, is put in the accusative case.

Thus, in Matt. 17, 4, καλόν ἐστιν (it is good) ἡμᾶς (us) ὧδε (here) εἶναι (to be), i.e., " it is good that we should be here " : ἡμᾶς is the accusative subject of the Infinitive εἶναι.

But if the subject of the Infinitive is the same person or thing as the subject of the preceding verb, the subject of the Infinitive is generally omitted, and any words qualifying the omitted subject are put in the nominative. Thus in Rom. 1, 22, φάσκοντες εἶναι σοφοί, " professing (themselves) to be wise " ; if this were fully expressed it would be φάσκοντες (professing) ἑαυτοὺς εἶναι σοφούς (themselves to be wise) ; but the same persons are the subject both of " professing " and " to be " ;

accordingly ἑαυτούς is omitted and σοφοί is put in the nominative.

Note the omission of the subject in the following, from Jas. 2, 14 : ἐὰν πίστιν λέγῃ τις ἔχειν, lit., "if anyone saith to have faith," i.e., saith he hath faith. Here τις, " anyone," is the subject of λέγῃ (pres. subjunc. after ἐάν, if), and the same person is the unexpressed subject of ἔχειν " (himself) to have." If it were expressed in full it would have to be ἐὰν πίστιν λέγῃ τις ἑαυτὸν ἔχειν (" himself to have ") —(not αὐτὸν ἔχειν [" him to have," which would mean some other person]). Because the person is the same subject for both verbs λέγῃ and ἔχειν, the accusative subject of ἔχειν is omitted. We must, however, insert it in English and say " If anyone saith he hath " (πίστιν is the accus. object of ἔχειν).

(2) The following is an example of the Infinitive as the object of the verb :—

2 Cor. 8, 11, νυνὶ δὲ (but now) καὶ (also) τὸ ποιῆσαι (the doing) ἐπιτελέσατε (complete). What tense of the Infinitive of ποιέω, I do, is ποιῆσαι ? Note its noun character with the article ; τὸ ποιῆσαι form together the object of the verb ἐπιτελέσατε: this is the 2nd pers. plur., 1st Aorist Imperative of ἐπιτελέω, I complete or fulfil. What is the force of the Aorist Imperative as distinct from the present ? (See Lesson XII, 2nd paragraph).

(3) In the following instances the Infinitive is governed by a preposition :—

H

Matt. 13, 5 : διὰ τὸ μὴ ἔχειν βάθος . . . διὰ τὸ μὴ ἔχειν ῥίζαν, " on-account-of the not having (lit., to have) depth . . . on-account-of the not having root." In each clause ἔχειν (the pres. Infinitive of ἔχω) is a verbal noun, used with the article τὸ. In English the verbal noun is " having "; so τὸ ἔχειν is " the having." When the preposition διὰ means " on account of " the noun governed by it is in the accusative case. Hence τὸ ἔχειν here is accusative. But ἔχειν is not only a noun, it is also a verb, and as such it governs its object βάθος in the accusative case (for the neuter noun βάθος see γένος, Lesson IX). The negative with the Infinitive is μή (not οὐ).

So also in the second clause, διὰ governs τὸ ἔχειν as a noun in the accusative case, and τὸ ἔχειν as a verb governs its object ῥίζαν, " a root," in the accusative case.

Matt. 20, 19 : εἰς τὸ ἐμπαῖξαι καὶ μαστιγῶσαι καὶ σταυρῶσαι, " to mock and scourge and crucify." The three verbs are, respectively, the first aorist Infinitive (see λῦσαι above) of ἐμπαίζω (future ἐμπαίξω), I mock, μαστιγόω (fut. μαστιγώσω), I scourge, and σταυρόω (fut. σταυρώσω), I crucify. The article τό goes with all three, and the article and the three infinitives are all governed in the accusative case by the preposition εἰς: literally " unto the to mock and to scourge and to crucify." The εἰς really signifies " with a view to," or " with the object of (mocking, etc.)."

(Other uses of the Infinitive will be explained later.

INFINITIVE MOOD SYNTAX

The above are sufficient to illustrate the force of this Mood.)

The student should go over very thoroughly the above examples of the Infinitive. After studying the notes, write out the English translations in a list, and then translate them back into the Greek text. This will help to overcome the difficulties of the Infinitive.

Exercise

Translate the following, with the help of the accompanying notes, learning first the words and their meanings.

(1) 2 Cor. 8, 11 ; νυνί, now : ὅπως, in order that : καθάπερ, just as : προθυμία, readiness : θέλω, I will.

Notes—τοῦ θέλειν is lit. " of the to will," i.e., " of the being willing " : this follows προθυμία, and so the translation is " readiness to will," the genitive of the Infinitive signifying intention or purpose.

(2) Luke 19, 27 : πλήν, howbeit : ἐχθρός, an enemy : θελήσαντας, accus. plur. masc., 1st aorist participle of θέλω, I wish, am willing, lit. " having been willing "—accus. in agreement with ἐχθρούς : βασιλεῦσαι, 1st aorist Infin. of βασιλεύω, I reign, lit. " me to reign" : ἐπ' for ἐπί, over : ἀγάγετε, 2nd pers. plur. Imperative of a 2nd aor. (see later) doubled syllable form of ἄγω, I bring : ὧδε, hither : κατασφάξατε, 1st aor. Imperative of κατασφάζω, I

105

slay : ἔμπροσθεν, before (takes the genitive case).

(3) Col. 1, 27, 28, from οἷς to Χριστῷ:—ἠθέλησεν, 3rd pers. sing., 1st aor. Indic. of θέλω, I am willing, I am pleased (this verb takes η for augment instead of ε) : γνωρίσαι, 1st aor. Infin. of γνωρίζω, I make known : πλοῦτος, wealth, riches (a neut. noun like γένος): ἔθνεσιν (dat. plur. of ἔθνος, a nation—here " Gentiles "—another neut. noun like γένος—dative case after ἐν): ἐλπίς, hope (genit. ἐλπίδος): καταγγέλλω, I proclaim (pronounced *katangello*) : νουθετοῦντες, nom. plur. masc. pres. participle of νουθετέω, I admonish—the ending -ουντες is contracted for -εοντες (see later) : διδάσκω, I teach : παραστήσωμεν, " we may present," subjunctive (for the form see later) : τέλειος, perfect.

(4) Rom. 15, 13 : ἐλπίδος [see under (3)] : πληρῶσαι, 3rd pers. sing. 1st aor. optative of πληρόω, I fill (the optative of a wish) : χαρᾶς, genit. of χαρά, joy (genitive is used after words of filling to signify " with "): πιστεύειν, Infin. as verbal noun, dative after ἐν—" in believing " (τῷ not to be translated): περισσεύειν, to abound—accus. of the Infin. verbal noun governed by εἰς : ὑμᾶς is the accus. subject of the Infin. (lit. " unto the you to abound "—i.e., " that ye may abound) : δύναμις, power : Ἅγιος, holy.

Re-translate the above four passages from English into Greek, correcting your result from the original.

SECOND AORIST ACTIVE

THE SECOND AORIST ACTIVE

Some verbs have a Second Aorist tense. Its meaning is the same as the First Aorist : it differs only in form. Very few verbs have both a First and Second Aorist : λύω has only the first. We shall therefore take as an example the verb τύπτω, I strike.

Note I—The endings of the Second Aorist Indicative are the same as those of the Imperfect, and as it is a past tense the augment is used. There is this difference in form, however, that the endings are added to the simple stem (see below).

Note II—In the other moods the endings are the same as those of the present tenses. Here again, the endings are added to the simple stem.

If the Present and Imperfect tenses have been thoroughly learnt there is no need to write out the Second Aorist forms in all the persons, save for the sake of practice. Remember that there is no augment except in the Indicative mood.

Second Aorist of τύπτω, I strike

Indicative, ἔτυπον, I struck
               (etc., see the Imperfect endings)
Imperative, τύπε, strike thou
               (etc., see the Present endings)
Subjunctive, τύπω, I (may) strike
               (etc., see the Present endings)
Optative, τύποιμι, I (might) strike
               (etc., see the Present endings)

Infinitive, τυπεῖν, to strike
Participle, τυπών, -οῦσα, -όν, having struck

It will be observed that the stem of the Present tense of τύπτω is τυπτ- but the stem of the second Aorist is τυπ-.

THE SECOND PERFECT

This tense is rare. It occurs only in the Active Voice and is simply a modified form of the Perfect. Thus, whereas the Perfect of τύπτω is τέτυφα, the 2nd Perfect is τέτυπα. Note the reduplication τε-, characteristic of all Perfect tenses.

LESSON XVI

Note for Revision—A complete paradigm of the Active Voice should be drawn up by the student from preceding Lessons, putting the Moods as headings of parallel columns, in the following order : Indicative, Imperative, Subjunctive, Optative, Infinitive, Participles ; and the names of the tenses down the left side —Present, Imperfect, Future, 1st Aorist, Perfect, Pluperfect, 2nd Aorist, remembering that the Imperfect and Pluperfect Tenses are found only in the Indicative Mood, and that there is no Future in the Imperative and Subjunctive.

The Passive Voice of the Verb

Whereas a verb is in the Active Voice when its subject is spoken of as acting or doing something, the Passive Voice signifies that the subject is acted upon. In English the Passive is formed by the use of the verb " to be " with the Passive Participle. Thus the Passive of " I loose " is " I am loosed " (always to be distinguished from the continuous tense of the Active Voice, formed by the verb " to be " with the Present Participle active, e.g., " I am loosing "). In Greek the Passive is formed (save in certain Perfect Tenses) simply by the addition of a different set of endings to the stem from those in the Active Voice.

The following are the Indicative Mood Tenses of the Passive Voice of λύω. The student must memorise them ; but only after being thoroughly familiar with the Active Voice forms.

The Passive Voice of λύω

INDICATIVE MOOD

Present Tense : " I am being loosed "

Singular

1st p. λύομαι (I am, etc.)
2nd p. λύῃ or λύει (thou art, etc.)
3rd p. λύεται (he is, etc.)

Plural

1st p. λυόμεθα (we are, etc.)
2nd p. λύεσθε (ye are, etc.)
3rd p. λύονται (they are, etc.)

Note the iota in the 2nd pers. sing. This form, λύῃ, is the same as the 3rd pers. sing., pres. subjunctive active. There is no difficulty in distinguishing them as to the meaning. The context makes that clear. The Active is " he may loose," the Passive " thou art being loosed."

INDICATIVE MOOD PASSIVE

Note that λυ- is the stem. The endings should be learnt apart from the stem.

Imperfect Tense : " I was being loosed," etc.

		Singular	Plural
1st	p.	ἐλυόμην	ἐλυόμεθα
2nd	p.	ἐλύου	ἐλύεσθε
3rd	p.	ἐλύετο	ἐλύοντο

Future Tense : " I shall be loosed "

		Singular	Plural
1st	p.	λυθήσομαι	λυθησόμεθα
2nd	p.	λυθήσῃ	λυθήσεσθε
3rd	p.	λυθήσεται	λυθήσονται

First Aorist : " I was loosed "

		Singular	Plural
1st	p.	ἐλύθην	ἐλύθημεν
2nd	p.	ἐλύθης	ἐλύθητε
3rd	p.	ἐλύθη	ἐλύθησαν

(*Note—The endings of the First Aorist Passive resemble the Imperfect of* εἰμί, *except in the 2nd and 3rd pers. sing.—see Lesson III. Observe the* -θ-, *characteristic of the Passive Voice, and the Augment*)

Perfect Tense : " I have been loosed "

		Singular	Plural
1st	p.	λέλυμαι	λελύμεθα
2nd	p.	λέλυσαι	λέλυσθε
3rd	p.	λέλυται	λέλυνται

111

GREEK TESTAMENT GRAMMAR

Pluperfect Tense : " I had been loosed "

	Singular	Plural
1st p.	ἐλελύμην	ἐλελύμεθα
2nd p.	ἐλέλυσο	ἐλέλυσθε
3rd p.	ἐλέλυτο	ἐλέλυντο

*Exercise on the Indicative Mood of the Passive
Voice*

*Translate the following sentences and passages,
after learning the vocabulary. Correct your rendering
from the R.V. text and re-translate from the English
into Greek.*

Vocabulary

μαρτύριον	witness	πτωχός-ή-όν	poor
ἄνομος	lawless	οὐρανός	heaven
τότε	then	πραΰς-εῖα-ύ	meek
σάρξ (gen. σαρκός)	flesh	δικαιοσύνη	righteous-ness
ἐντολή	command-ment	ἐλεήμων	(neut. -ον), merciful
μακάριος-α-ον	blessed		

(1) ὅτι (because) ἐπιστεύθη (1st aor. indic. passive
of πιστεύω, I believe) τὸ μαρτύριον ἡμῶν ἐφ' ὑμᾶς (2
Thess. 1, 10). The subject of the verb is τὸ
μαρτύριον ἡμῶν. Note that ἐφ' is for ἐπί, " unto "
(not " among," as A.V.) : the ι is dropped before
the υ of ὑμᾶς and then the π becomes φ because of
the rough breathing, the ʽ. To say ἐπ' ὑμᾶς would
be awkward : hence the π becomes aspirated to φ.

112

(2) καὶ τότε ἀποκαλυφθήσεται (future passive of ἀποκαλύπτω, I reveal) ὁ ἄνομος (2 Thess. 2, 8).

(3) John 1, 13 : ἐξ is for ἐκ, "of," the κ becoming ξ before the αἱ of αἱμάτων). Note this gen. plur., lit., "bloods" : αἷμα and θέλημα are declined like πνεῦμα (Lesson IX). For ἀνδρός see Lesson VIII. ἐγεννήθησαν is 3rd plur. 1st aor. pass. of γεννάω, I beget (passive "am born"). The change from α in γεννάω to η will be explained later.

(4) John 14, 21. Note the pres. participles of ἔχω, I have, τηρέω, I keep, ἀγαπάω, I love. Note the difference between the future passive ἀγαπηθήσεται (3rd pers.) and the future active ἀγαπήσω (1st pers.) : ὑπό is "by"—it takes the genitive : κἀγώ is short for καὶ ἐγώ : ἐμφανίσω is the future of ἐμφανίζω, I manifest. It would be well to commit this verse to memory.

(5) Matt. 5, 3-7. Study carefully the following notes. The verb "to be" is often omitted ; εἰσίν, "are," is to be understood after μακάριοι : τῷ πνεύματι is dative of the point in which an adjective (here πτωχοί, poor) is applied ; hence we must say "poor in spirit" (the article must not be translated) : αὐτῶν, "of them," i.e., "theirs" ; πενθοῦντες is the pres. participle, nom. plur. masc. of πενθέω, I mourn, for πενθέοντες, the εο contracting to ου : παρακληθήσονται is 3rd pers. plur., future, indic. passive of παρακαλέω, I comfort : κληρονομήσουσιν is the fut. active of κληρονομέω, I inherit : πεινῶντες, is the nom. plur., masc., pres.

participle of πεινάω, I hunger, for πεινάοντες, the αο contracting to ω : so διψῶντες is from διψάω, I thirst : χορτασθήσονται is 3rd plur. fut. passive of χορτάζω, I fill, satisfy (verbs in -ζω take σ in fut. and 1st aor.) : ἐλεηθήσονται is fut. passive of ἐλεέω, I show mercy.

IMPERATIVE MOOD, PASSIVE VOICE

Present Tense

	Singular	Plural	
2nd p.	λύου, be thou loosed	λύεσθε	be ye loosed
3rd p.	λυέσθω, let him (her, it) be loosed	λυέσθωσαν or λυέσθων	let them be loosed

Aorist Tense : " Be thou loosed (at once) "

	Singular	Plural
2nd p.	λύθητι	λύθητε
3rd p.	λυθήτω	λυθήτωσαν

Perfect Tense

(expressing continuance of a past act)

	Singular	Plural
2nd p.	λέλυσο	λέλυσθε
3rd p.	λελύσθω	λελύσθωσαν or λελύσθων

Students should now obtain a copy of the little Greek-English Lexicon to the New Testament, by A. Souter. This is published by The Clarendon

Press, Oxford. It is one of the best books of reference published in connection with Greek Testament study, and forms a good companion to Nestle's Text. Being small in size it is handy for taking about. In the course of the next few lessons this book will be substituted for the vocabularies given in the exercises.

LESSON XVII

Exercise on the Imperative Mood

Learn the following vocabulary. Then translate the passages with the help of the notes. Re-translate into the Greek, correcting your result.

Vocabulary

κόκκος	grain	θάλασσα	sea
σίναπι	(gen. εως)	καρδία	heart
	mustard (declined like πόλις, Lesson IX)	περισσῶς	exceedingly

(1) Luke 17, 6 : ἔχετε is 2nd pers., plur., pres. indic. of ἔχω : ἐλέγετε ἄν is " ye would say " (this construction of the imperfect with ἄν is explained later) : Ἐκριζώθητι, 2nd per., sing., 1st aor. imperative passive of ἐκριζόω, I root up ; φυτεύθητι, the same form from φυτεύω, I plant : ὑπήκουσεν ἄν, " it would obey "— 1st aor. active of ὑπακούω, note that the augment is formed by the change of the α of ἀκούω into η, ὑπ being for ὑπό, a preposition compounded with the verb ἀκούω. The preposition does not augment, the main verb does. Note the datives in this verse, one after λέγω, the other after ἐν.

116

SUBJUNCTIVE MOOD PASSIVE

(2) John 14, 1 : ταρασσέσθω is 3rd pers., sing., pres. imperative, passive of ταράσσω, I trouble : πιστεύετε may be 2nd pers. plur. of either the pres. indic. active or the pres. imperative active of πιστεύω, i.e., either "believe ye" or "ye believe."

(3) λέγουσιν πάντες Σταυρωθήτω. This verb is the 1st aor. imperative of σταυρόω, I crucify, i.e., "let Him be crucified" (see λυθήτω, above). This sentence is from Matt. 27, 22 (end of verse) ; translate verse 23 : ὁ δέ is "but he," ἔφη, "said." What tense of ποιέω is ἐποίησεν ? ἔκραζον is 3rd pers., plur., imperf. indic. active of κράζω, I cry out, "they kept on crying out."

(4) 1 Cor. 11, 6-8 : κατακαλύπτεται, 3rd pers., sing., pres. indic., passive of κατακαλύπτω, I cover up, veil (for the form see λύομαι) : γυνή, "a woman," an irregular noun of the 3rd declension (its acc., gen., dat., sing. are γυναῖκα, γυναικός, γυναικί, and the plural cases are γυναῖκες, γυναῖκας, γυναικῶν, γυναιξί) : κειράσθω, 3rd pers., sing., aor. imperative, middle, of κείρω, I shear, "let her be shorn."

THE SUBJUNCTIVE MOOD, PASSIVE VOICE

Present Tense : " I may be loosed " (a process)

1st p.	λύωμαι	λυώμεθα
2nd p.	λύῃ	λύησθε
3rd p.	λύηται	λύωνται

117

Note the long vowel, characteristic of the subjunctive present, etc. Also the iota subscript in the 2nd pers. sing.

First Aorist : " *I may be loosed* " (*a definite act*)

1st p.	λυθῶ	λυθῶμεν
2nd p.	λυθῇς	λυθῆτε
3rd p.	λυθῇ	λυθῶσι(ν)

Note the endings, like the subjunctive of εἰμί; *see Lesson XIII.*

Perfect Tense : " *I may have been loosed.*"

This tense is formed by the perfect participle (*see later*), *with the subjunctive of the verb* εἰμί ; *thus the literal meaning would be* " (*that*) *I may be having been loosed,*" *but the literal meaning must not be pressed.*

1st p.	λελυμένος ὦ	λελυμένοι ὦμεν
2nd p.	λελυμένος ᾖς	λελυμένοι ἦτε
3rd p.	λελυμένος ᾖ	λελυμένοι ὦσι(ν)

Note—The λελυμένος, being a participle, is also an adjective, and therefore must agree in gender and number with the subject : λελυμένος-η-ον is declined like a 2nd declension adjective. Note, e.g., the -οι of the plural. This would be -αι if women were spoken of.

Exercise on the Subjunctive Mood of the Passive Voice.

Before doing this exercise it will be necessary for the student to revise the five principal uses of the Subjunctive mood as given in Lesson XIII.

SUBJUNCTIVE MOOD PASSIVE

Translate the passages with the help of the notes, learning the meanings of new words.· Re-translate into the Greek and correct from the Text.

I—Containing instances of the Subjunctive, Passive, in clauses of *Purpose* (see Lesson XIII, *I*).

(1) 2 Cor. 9, 3 : ἔπεμψα, 1st aor. indic., active of πέμπω, I send : ἵνα μή, "in order that . . . not " : τὸ καύχημα ἡμῶν τὸ ὑπερ ὑμῶν, lit., " the boasting of us (i.e., our boasting) the (i.e., the [boasting]) on behalf of you" ; we may render by " our boasting, that, namely, on your behalf " : κενωθῇ (1st aor. subjunc., passive of κενόω, I make void), " may (not) be made void " : ἔλεγον (1st per. sing., imperf. indic., active of λέγω) " I was saying " : παρεσκευασμένοι ἦτε, 2nd pers., plur., perf. subjunc., passive, of παρασκευάζω, I prepare ; this is composed of the preposition παρά and the verb σκευάζω ; verbs beginning with two consonants (except a mute and a liquid) reduplicate by a simple ε ; hence παρα becomes παρε- as with the ordinary augment when a preposition is prefixed to a verb.

(2) ὅπως ἂν ἀποκαλυφθῶσιν ἐκ πολλῶν καρδιῶν διαλογισμοί (Luke 2, 35, last sentence) : ὅπως, ". in order that " ; ἄν, not to be translated ; ἀποκαλυφθῶσιν, 3rd pers., plur., 1st aor. subjunc., passive of ἀποκαλύπτω, I reveal, agreeing with its subject διαλογισμοί, " thoughts " ; ἐκ can simply be

rendered " of " ; it takes the genitive, πολλῶν (see Lesson VII).

II—Containing instances of the Subjunctive Passive in *Conditional Clauses* (see Lesson XIII, *II*).

(1) John 12, 31-32 : κρίσις, judgment ; κόσμος, world ; ἄρχων, prince, ruler ; ἐκβληθήσεται, 3rd pers., sing., fut. indic., passive of ἐκβάλλω, I cast out (an irregular verb) ; ἔξω, out (an adverb) ; κἀγώ for καὶ ἐγώ ; ὑψωθῶ, 1st aor. subjunc., passive of ὑψόω, I lift up ; ἕλκω, I draw ; πρός, to.

(2) 2 Cor. 5, 1 : οἴδαμεν, we know (irregular) : ἐπίγειος, -α, -ον, earthly ; οἰκία, house ; σκῆνος, tabernacle, tent (3rd declension, neut. like γένος, genit. -ους) ; καταλυθῇ, 1st aor. subjunc., pass. of καταλύω, I loosen down, take down (of a tent), dissolve ; οἰκοδομή, a building ; ἀχειροποίητος, not-hand-made (the prefix ἀ- signifies a negative ; χείρ, the hand ; ποιητός, a verbal adjective, " made "—hence " not made with hands ").

III—Containing an instance of the Subjunctive Passive in *Relative Clauses* (see Lesson XIII, *III*).

Mark 14, 9 : ὅπου, " where "—ὅπου ἐάν together make " wherever," introducing an indefinite relative clause, i.e., a relative clause expressing indefiniteness—the ἐάν must not be translated here by " if," it simply adds the idea of indefinite locality to ὅπου ; κηρυχθῇ, 3rd pers. sing., 1st aor. subjunc., passive of κηρύσσω, I preach—translate by " is preached " (not " was preached " ; the aorist in the subjunctive mood is not necessarily a past tense, here it points to the preaching as a precise announcement)—note the subjunctive in a relative clause with ἐάν, " wherever the gospel is preached ": καί, also ; λαληθήσεται, fut. indic., passive of λαλέω, I speak ; εἰς " unto " or " for " ; μνημόσυνον, a memorial.

IV—Containing an instance of the *Deliberative Subjunctive* (see Lesson XIII, *IV*).

Matt. 26, 54 : πῶς, how ; οὖν, therefore ; πληρωθῶσιν, 3rd pers. plur., 1st aor. subjunc., passive of πληρόω, I fulfil, agreeing with its subject γραφαί ; γραφή, a writing, scripture ; οὕτως, thus ; δεῖ, it is necessary ; γενέσθαι, " to become " (an irregular verb—see later).

V—The use of the Subjunctive Passive in *Exhortations* is very rare (see Lesson XIII, *V*).

LESSON XVIII

OPTATIVE MOOD, PASSIVE VOICE

Present Tense : " I might be loosed," etc.

	Singular	Plural
1st p.	λυοίμην	λυοίμεθα
2nd p.	λύοιο	λύοισθε
3rd p.	λύοιτο	λύοιντο

Future Tense : " I should be loosed "

	Singular	Plural
1st p.	λυθησοίμην	λυθησοίμεθα
2nd p.	λυθήσοιο	λυθήσοισθε
3rd p.	λυθήσοιτο	λυθήσοιντο

First Aorist : " I might be (or am to be) loosed "

	Singular	Plural
1st p.	λυθείην	λυθείημεν
2nd p.	λυθείης	λυθείητε
3rd p.	λυθείη	λυθεῖεν

Perfect : " I might have been loosed "

	Singular	Plural
1st p.	λελυμένος εἴην	λελυμένοι εἴημεν
2nd p.	λελυμένος εἴης	λελυμένοι εἴητε
3rd p.	λελυμένος εἴη	λελυμένοι εἴησαν

122

OPTATIVE MOOD PASSIVE

The Optative Passive is very rare. No exercise therefore will be given upon it.

THE INFINITIVE MOOD, PASSIVE VOICE

Pres. Infin.	λύεσθαι,	to be loosed
Future	λυθήσεσθαι,	to be about to be loosed
First Aor.	λυθῆναι,	to be loosed (at once)
Perfect	λελύσθαι,	to have been loosed

Exercise on the Infinitive Passive

Before doing this exercise revise the Notes on the Infinitive Mood at the end of Lesson XIV.

Study the accompanying notes, and learn the meanings of new words; after translating, re-translate as usual.

(1) 1 Cor. 10, 13, from πιστὸς δὲ ὁ Θεός to τὴν ἔκβασιν: πιστὸς, faithful; εᾶσει, 3rd pers. sing., fut. indic., of ἐάω, I permit, allow; πειρασθῆναι, 1st aor. infin., passive, of πειράζω, I tempt; ὑπέρ, above; ὅ, acc., neut., sing., of ὅς; δύνασθε, ye are able; πειρασμός, a temptation; ἔκβασις, a way of escape.

(2) Mark 14, 28: note particularly the phrase μετὰ τὸ ἐγερθῆναί με—the preposition μετὰ is "after," it governs the whole of the rest of the phrase in the accusative case; the article τό describes the phrase ἐγερθῆναί με, which, literally, is "me to be raised," the verb being the 1st aor. infin., passive, of ἐγείρω, I raise. These two words form the construction known as the Accusative

with the Infinitive, which will be explained later. Accordingly τὸ ἐγερθῆναί με is "the me to be raised." Literally, then, the whole phrase is "after the Me to be raised," i.e., "after the [event] that I am raised," and hence we must translate by "after I am raised," for that is the corresponding idiom in English ; προάξω, fut. of προάγω, I go before.

(3) Matt. 3, 14 : διεκώλυεν, 3rd pers. sing., imperf. indic., of διακωλύω, I hinder—"he was hindering" (note the augment, the compounded preposition διά changing to διε) ; βαπτισθῆναι, 1st aor., infin. passive of βαπτίζω ; ἔρχῃ, comest (an irregular verb).

(4) Acts 14, 9 : ἤκουεν, imperfect of ἀκούω, I hear, which takes the genitive case (τοῦ Παύλου) —note that ἀ- make augment ἠ-. The τοῦ is not to be translated ; the article often goes with a proper name ; λαλοῦντος, gen., sing., masc., pres. participle of λαλέω, I speak—for λαλέοντος (εο becomes ου) ; ἀτενίσας, nom., sing., masc., 1st aor. partic. of ἀτενίζω, I look steadfastly ; ἰδών, seeing (explained later) ; σωθῆναι, 1st aor. infin., pass. of σώζω, I save : the τοῦ is not to be translated —τοῦ σωθῆναι is a genitive construction after πίστιν, faith, lit., "faith of the to be saved," i.e., "faith to be saved."

THE PARTICIPLES OF THE PASSIVE VOICE

Note—These are verbal adjectives, like those

of the active voice. They are declined like adjectives, the particular form agreeing in case, number and gender with the noun or pronoun to which the participle refers.

Present Participle : " being loosed "

Masc. λυόμενος, Fem. λυομένη, Neut. λυόμενον
This is declined, singular and plural, like ἀγαθός (see Lesson IV).

Future Participle : " about to be loosed "

M. λυθησόμενος, F. λυθησομένη, N. λυθησόμενον

First Aorist Participle : " Having been loosed "

Masc. λυθείς, Fem. λυθεῖσα, Neut. λυθέν
This is declined like ἑκών, ἑκοῦσα, ἑκόν (Lesson IX), -ε- taking the place of -ο- in the masc. and neut. in all cases except the nom. sing. masc., and dat. plur., and -ει- taking the place of -ου- in the fem. and in all genders in the dat. plural.

Thus the accusative singular is λυθέντα, λυθεῖσαν, λυθέν, and the genitive λυθέντος, λυθείσης, λυθέντος, the dat. plural is λυθεῖσι, λυθείσαις, λυθε ῖσι.

Perfect Participle : " having been loosened "

Masc. λελυμένος, Fem. λελυμένη, Neut. λελυμένον

Exercise

Translate the following passages, with the help of the accompanying notes, learning the meaning of new words and retranslating into the Greek.

(1) Rom. 8, 24 : τῇ . . . ἐλπίδι is dat. of instrument, " by hope " ; ἐσώθημεν, 1st pers. plur., 1st aor., indic. passive, of σώζω, I save ; βλεπομένη, nom., sing., fem., pres. partic., passive, of βλέπω, I see, " being seen " ; ὁ neut. of ὅς; ; τις, anyone.

(2) Matt. 27, 37 : ἐπέθηκαν, they put up (a form explained later) ; ἐπάνω, above (a preposition taking the genitive) ; κεφαλή, a head ; αἰτία, an accusation (here the accus. object of the verb ἐπέθηκεν); γεγραμμένην, acc., sing., fem., perf. partic., passive, of γράφω, I write, " having been written," or simply " written " (the root of γράφω is γραπ-, and γεγραπμένην becomes γεγραμμένην, the π assimilating to the μ for the sake of sound).

(3) Luke 7, 8, as far as στρατιώτας : καί, also ; ὑπό, under ; ἐξουσία, authority ; τασσόμενος, nom., sing., masc., pres. partic., passive, of τάσσω I set, " being set " ; στρατιώτης, a soldier (like μαθητής, Lesson III).

(4) Matt. 2, 14-15 : ὁ δέ, but he ; ἐγερθείς, nom., sing., masc., 1st aor., partic. passive, of ἐγείρω, I arouse, awake, lit., "having been aroused," παρέλαβεν " took " (an irregular verb) ; παιδίον, a little child ; νυκτός, by night, genitive of νύξ (genitive of time) ; ἀνεχώρησεν, 3rd pers. sing., 1st aor. indic., active, of ἀναχωρέω, I depart (note the augment -ε- in the preposition ἀνε) ; ἐκεῖ, there ; ἕως, until ; τελευτή, an end, or death ; πληρωθῇ, 3rd pers. sing., 1st aor. subj.,

passive, of πληρόω, I fulfil ; ῥηθέν, nom., sing.,
neut., 1st aor. partic., passive, of ῥέω, I utter,
speak (see λυθείς, λυθεῖσα, λυθέν, above) ; διά, by
means of (takes the genitive).

THE SECOND AORIST PASSIVE

The tense endings are the same as those of
the first aorist throughout the moods (save in
one ending) but the ending is added to the simple
root and without the -θ-. Thus, whereas the
first aorist indic. passive of τύπτω, I strike, is
ἐτύφθην, etc., the second aorist is ἐτύπην, etc. The
only exception is in the 2nd pers. sing., imperative,
where -θι is found instead of -τι.

The following will be sufficient. The student
who has learnt the first aorist tenses will readily
supply the full second aorist from memory.
They should at all events be written out in full.
The meanings are the same.

Indicative,	ἐτύπην
Imperative,	τύπηθι (3rd p. s. τυπήτω)
Subjunctive,	τυπῶ
Optative,	τυπείην
Infinitive,	τυπῆναι
Participle,	τυπείς, -εῖσα, -έν

THE MIDDLE VOICE

Whereas in English there are only two voices,

active and passive, the Greek language has three. The Middle Voice chiefly signifies that a person has a special interest in the effects of his action, that he is acting either upon, or for, himself, or that when he is acting for others he has a personal interest in their condition or welfare. Sometimes, however, it is scarcely possible to distinguish in meaning between the middle and the active. Examples are given below.

In four tenses of the middle voice the forms are the same as those of the passive. These are the present, imperfect, perfect and pluperfect. Accordingly for the paradigm of these the student is referred to the passive voice (Lesson XVI). The future and aorist tenses are different.

MIDDLE VOICE—INDICATIVE MOOD

For the four following tenses see the passive voice : *Present*, λύομαι etc., " I am loosing myself (or, for myself) " ; *Imperfect*, ἐλυόμην, etc., " I was loosing myself (or for myself) " ; *Perfect*, λέλυμαι, etc., " I have loosed myself (or for myself) " ; *Pluperfect*, ἐλελύμην, etc., " I had, etc."

Future : " *I will loose myself (or for, etc.)* "

Singular		Plural
1st p.	λύσομαι	λυσόμεθα
2nd p.	λύσῃ	λύσεσθε
3rd p.	λύσεται	λύσονται

128

THE MIDDLE VOICE

First Aorist : " *I loosed myself (or for, etc.)* "

1st p.	ἐλυσάμην	ἐλυσάμεθα
2nd p.	ἐλύσω	ἐλύσασθε
3rd p.	ἐλύσατο	ἐλύσαντο

IMPERATIVE MOOD

For the two following tenses see the Passive Voice : *Present,* λύου, etc., "loose thyself (or for thyself) " ; *Perfect,* λέλυσο, etc., " have loosed thyself (or for thyself)," etc. There is no imperfect or pluperfect outside the indicative, nor any future in the imperative and subjunctive.

First Aorist : " *loose thyself (or for thyself)*
at once "

	Singular	Plural
2nd p.	λῦσαι	λύσασθε
3rd p.	λυσάσθω	λυσάσθωσαν or λυσάσθων

SUBJUNCTIVE MOOD

For the two following tenses see the Passive Voice : *Present,* λύωμαι, etc., " I may loose myself (or for myself) " ; *Perfect,* λελυμένος ὦ, etc., " I may have loosed myself (or for myself)."

First Aorist : " *I may loose myself (or for*
myself) "

	Singular	Plural
1st p.	λύσωμαι	λυσώμεθα
2nd p.	λύσῃ	λύσησθε
3rd p.	λύσηται	λύσωνται

129

LESSON XIX

MIDDLE VOICE—OPTATIVE MOOD

For the two following tenses see the Passive Voice : *Present,* λυοίμην, etc., " I might loose myself (or for myself) " ; *Perfect,* λελυμένος εἴην, etc., " I might have loosed myself (or for myself)."

Future : " *I should loose myself (or for myself)* "

Singular		Plural	
1st p.	λυσοίμην	λυσοίμεθα	
2nd p.	λύσοιο	λύσοισθε	
3rd p.	λύσοιτο	λύσοιντο	

First Aorist : " *I might loose myself (or for myself)* "

1st p.	λυσαίμην	λυσαίμεθα
2nd p.	λύσαιο	λύσαισθε
3rd p.	λύσαιτο	λύσαιντο

INFINITIVE MOOD

Present (like the Passive), λύεσθαι, " to loose oneself (or for oneself) " ; *Perfect* (like the *Passive*), λελύσθαι, " to have loosed oneself (or for oneself)."

130

THE MIDDLE VOICE

Future, λύσεσθαι, " to be about to loose oneself (or for oneself)."

First Aorist, λύσασθαι, " to loose oneself (or for oneself) immediately."

PARTICIPLES

Present (like the Passive), λυόμενος-η-ον, etc., " loosing oneself (or for oneself) "; *Perfect* (like the Passive) λελυμένος-η-ον, etc., " having loosed oneself (or for oneself)." *Future*, λυσόμενος-η-ον, " being about to loose oneself (etc.)." *First Aorist*, λυσάμενος-η-ον, " having loosed oneself (or for oneself) immediately."

The student should compare and contrast the above Futures and First Aorists in the various Moods with those of the Passive Voice, noting carefully the differences. They should be written out in parallel columns from memory.

Exercise on the Middle Voice

Translate the following passages with the help of the accompanying notes, learning new words and re-translating into Greek.

(1) Jas. 4, 3: αἰτεῖτε, 2nd pers. plur., pres. indic., active of αἰτέω, I ask (for αἰτέετε: -εε- contracts to -ει-) ; λαμβάνω, I receive ; διότι, because ; κακῶς, evilly, amiss ; αἰτεῖσθε (for αἰτέεσθε), same person, number, tense and mood as αἰτεῖτε, but middle voice, " ye ask for yourselves " (note the purposive change, stressing the selfishness) ; ἡδονή, pleasure ;

δαπανήσητε, 1st aor. subjunc., of δαπανάω, I spend.

(2) Acts 22, 16 : τί, why ? μέλλεις, 2nd sing., pres. indic., of μέλλω, I delay, tarry ; ἀναστάς, " having arisen " (an aor. partic., explained later) ; βάπτισαι, 2nd pers. sing., 1st aor., imperative, middle, of βαπτίζω, lit., " get thyself baptised " ; ἀπόλουσαι, same tense and voice of ἀπολούω, I wash away, "get (thy sins) washed away " ; ἐπικαλεσάμενος, 1st aor. participle, middle, of ἐπικαλέω, I call upon, " calling for thyself upon . . ." Note the force of all these aorists, implying decisive and immediate action, the middle voice signifying, in the first two instances, that Saul was to arrange for the thing to be done.

(3) Mark 7, 3, 4 : πυγμῇ, a fist (the dative here signifies " with the fist," an idiom used of washing ; to wash with the fist was to wash " diligently "); νίψωνται, 3rd pers. plur., 1st aor. subjunc., middle, of νίπτω, I wash—conditional subjunctive after ἐὰν μὴ, " if not," i.e., " unless "; χείρ, a hand (fem.) ; ἐσθίω, I eat ; κρατοῦντες, for κρατέοντες, nom., plur., masc., pres. partic., of κρατέω, I hold fast ; παράδοσις a tradition (declined like πόλις) ; πρεσβύτερος, an elder ; ἀπ', for ἀπό (with genit.) ; ἀγορά, a market place ; ῥαντίσωνται, 1st aor. subjunc., middle, of ῥαντίζω, I sprinkle (note the force of the middle voice in each case, intimating zealous self-interest in washing and sprinkling) ; ἄλλα, neut., plur., of ἄλλος, other,

" other things " (distinguish this from ἀλλά " but ") ; ἐστιν, though singular, must be translated " are," owing to the rule that *when the subject of a verb is in the neuter plural the verb is put in the singular.* Here we must render by " there are " ; παρέλαβον, " they received " (an irregular verb) ; κρατεῖν, pres. infin. ; for ποτήριον, ξέστης and χαλκίον see Souter's Lexicon.

(4) Matt. 20, 1 : ὅμοιος, -α, -ον, like ; for βασιλεία and οἰκοδεσπότης see Souter ; ὅστις, who ; ἐξῆλθεν, " went out " (an irregular verb) ; ἅμα πρωΐ, lit. "together early," i.e., " early in the morning " ; μισθώσασθαι, 1st aor. infin., middle, of μισθόω, I hire (infinitive of purpose), " to hire for himself."

(5) Col. 4, 5 : περιπατεῖτε (for περιπατέετε), 2nd pers. plur., pres. imperative, active of περιπατέω, I walk ; ἔξω, without ; ἐξαγοραζόμενοι, nom., plur., masc., pres. participle, middle, of ἐξαγοράζω, I buy up, " buying up for yourselves."

(6) Mark 9, 8 : ἐξάπινα, suddenly ; περιβλεψάμενοι, 1st aor. participle, middle, of περιβλέπω, I look around (περί, around, βλέπω, I look)— " having looked around " — the middle voice expresses, in a way that cannot well be brought out in English, their deep interest : οὐκέτι, no longer ; οὐδένα, accus. of οὐδείς, nobody ; εἶδον, " they saw " (an irregular verb) ; μόνον, alone ; μεθ' for μετά (when this preposition takes the genitive it denotes " with ").

Note—The student should become familiar with the whole of the regular verb λύω in the three voices, Active, Middle and Passive. This will greatly facilitate the reading of the Greek Testament. To help towards the thorough acquisition of the regular verb it will be well to write out in full from memory (correcting the result if necessary) the various tense endings of the following regular verb on the model of λύω:—:—βουλεύω, I advise (the meaning of this in the middle voice is " to advise oneself," that is, " to deliberate ").

DEPONENT VERBS

These are the verbs which have no active voice, but are either middle or passive in form, though they are active in meaning. They were called Deponent from the Latin verb " *deponere,*" to lay aside, as they are considered to lay aside passive meanings.

The following are very common and should be committed to memory, especially the various irregular forms of the tenses mentioned.

βούλομαι, I will, wish, purpose; imperf. ἐβουλόμην; ; 1st aor. ἐβουλήθην.

ἀποκρίνομαι, I answer; for the past tense " I answered," either the 1st aor. passive, ἀπεκρίθην is used (and this is the usual form), or the 1st aor. middle, ἀπεκρινάμην. Thus " he answered " is usually ἀπεκρίθη, but in seven places we find ἀπεκρίνατο.

γίνομαι, I become; imperf. ἐγινόμην ; fut.

DEPONENT VERBS

γενήσομαι ; 1st aor. (passive in form) ἐγενήθην ; perfect γεγένημαι. There is a perfect with an active form, γέγονα, and with the same meaning, " I have become " ; there is also a 2nd aor., ἐγενόμην, " I became," with the same endings as in the imperfect. This 2nd aor. is common in the 3rd pers. sing., optative, γένοιτο, in the phrase μὴ γένοιτο, " let it not be," translated " God forbid."

δέχομαι, I receive ; 1st aor. ἐδεξάμην ; perf. δέδεγμαι.

λογίζομαι, I reckon ; 1st aor. ἐλογισάμην, I reckoned ; 1st aor. pass. ἐλογίσθην, I was reckoned.

ἄρχομαι, I begin ; fut. ἄρξομαι ; 1st aor. ἠρξάμην.

ἔρχομαι, I come ; imperf. ἠρχόμην ; other forms are irregular, as follows :—future ἐλεύσομαι ; perfect ἐλήλυθα; ; 2nd aor. ἦλθον.

Exercise on the Deponent Verbs

(1) Translate the first nine verses of the Gospel of John, noting the following :—In ver. 3, δι' is for διά, by ; ἐγένετο is 3rd pers. sing., 2nd aor. of γίνομαι (see list above), and, though plural in meaning is singular, as it has a neuter plural subject πάντα, all things—" all things became (or came to be)." The next ἐγένετο is singular in agreement with ἕν, one thing (ἕν is the neut. of the numeral εἷς, μία, ἕν, masc., fem., neut., " one ") ; οὐδέ is " not even."—ἐγένετο οὐδὲ ἕν, "not even one thing came to be " (distinguish the numeral ἕν from the preposition ἐν,

in); ὅ, neut. of the rel. pron. ὅς, which; γέγονεν, 3rd pers. sing., perf., of γίνομαι, hath come to be; in ver. 5 κατέλαβεν, comprehended, is an irregular verb, to be learnt later. In ver. 6 translate ἐγένετο by " there was "; ἀπεσταλμένος, sent (for this perfect participle see later); παρά with genit., " from." In ver. 7 ἦλθεν is 3rd pers. sing., 2nd aor. of ἔρχομαι (see above); εἰς, unto (i.e., " for "); μαρτυρήσῃ, 1st aor. subjunc. of μαρτυρέω; περί, concerning; πιστεύσωσιν, 1st aor. subj. In ver. 9 πάντα is acc., sing., masc., " every "; ἐρχόμενον, nom., sing., neut., pres. partic., " coming "—this agrees and goes with φῶς (neut.), not with ἄνθρωπον.

(2) Translate John 1, 47-49 : εἶδεν, saw— an irregular 2nd aorist (see later), Ἴδε, behold ; ἀληθῶς, truly ; Πόθεν, whence ? γινώσκεις, 2nd pers. sing., pres. indic. of γινώσκω, I know ; ἀπεκρίθη, 3rd pers. sing., 1st aor. indic. (passive in form) of ἀποκρίνομαι (see list above) ; this takes the dative " (answered) to him." Study carefully the phrase Πρὸ τοῦ σε Φίλιππον φωνῆσαι, with the help of the following remarks, and see notes on the Infinitive, Lesson XV—πρό, before (a preposition taking the genitive) ; τοῦ (this article, genitive case after πρό, is not to be translated ; it qualifies the whole phrase that follows) ; σε, thee, is the object of φωνῆσαι (" called thee ") ; φωνῆσαι is the 1st aor., infin. of φωνέω, I call, lit. " to have called " ; the subject of the infinitive is Φίλιππον (for this construction

of the accus. with the infin. see Lesson XVIII, p. 123) ; this phrase σε φωνῆσαι Φίλιππον is, lit., " Philip to have called thee " ; this whole phrase, with its article τοῦ, is governed by πρό; literally, therefore, we have " Before Philip to have called thee." The only way to translate this concise idiomatic phrase is " Before Philip called thee " ; ὄντα is acc. sing., masc., of ὤν the pres. partic. of εἰμί (see Lesson IX) " being " (i.e., " when thou wast ") ; ὑπό, under ; εἶδον, I saw. In ver. 49 the τοῦ before Ἰσραήλ is not to be translated, as the article is generally used with a proper noun.

LESSON XX

Verbs with Contracted Vowel Endings

Note—Contractions take place only in the present and imperfect tenses. All other tenses, since they have no two vowels coming together, are formed regularly, taking, however, a long vowel in the last syllable but one (see below).

When α, ε, ο precede a vowel, whether long or short, it is generally contracted into one syllable. This has been illustrated in nouns and adjectives with contracted vowels (see Lesson VII). There are three forms of verbs, those with α— stems, e.g., τιμάω (τιμῶ), stem τιμα—, I honour; those with ε— stems, e.g., φιλέω (φιλῶ), stem φιλε —, I love ; those with ο— stems, e.g., δηλόω (δηλῶ), stem δηλο—, I manifest.

In the following paradigms the uncontracted forms are given in brackets. The contracted forms should be memorised.

(τιμάω) τιμῶ, I honour

CONTRACTED VERBS WITH —α— STEMS
ACTIVE VOICE
INDICATIVE MOOD

138

CONTRACTED VERBS

Present Tense

1st p.	(τιμάω) τιμῶ	(τιμάομεν) τιμῶμεν
2nd p.	(τιμάεις) τιμᾷς	(τιμάετε) τιμᾶτε
3rd p.	(τιμάει) τιμᾷ	(τιμάουσι) τιμῶσι

Imperfect Tense

1st p.	(ἐτίμαον) ἐτίμων	(——ομεν) ἐτιμῶμεν
2nd p.	(——ες) ἐτίμας	(——ετε) ἐτιμᾶτε
3rd p.	(——ε) ἐτίμα	(——ον) ἐτίμων

IMPERATIVE MOOD
Present Tense

2nd p.	(τίμαε) τίμα	(τιμάετε) τιμᾶτε
3rd p.	(——έτω) τιμάτω	(——έτωσαν) τιμάτωσαν

SUBJUNCTIVE MOOD

The present tense is exactly like the indicative present, owing to the contractions.

OPTATIVE MOOD
Present Tense

1st p.	(τιμάοιμι) τιμῷμι	(——οιμεν) τιμῷμεν
2nd p.	(——οις) τιμῷς	(——οιτε) τιμῷτε
3rd p.	(——οι) τιμῷ	(——οιεν) τιμῷεν

Note that the iota becomes subscript in each person. There is an alternative and more usual form for this tense, as follows :—

1st p.	τιμῴην	——ημεν
2nd p.	——ης	——ητε
3rd p.	——η	——ησαν

INFINITIVE MOOD (*Present*)
(τιμάειν) τιμᾶν

PARTICIPLE (*Present*)

Masc.	Fem.	Neut.
(τιμάων) τιμῶν,	(τιμάουσα) τιμῶσα,	(τιμάον) τιμῶν

139

GREEK TESTAMENT GRAMMAR

Passive and Middle Voices
Indicative Mood
Present Tense

1st p. (τιμάομαι) τιμῶμαι   (——όμεθα) τιμώμεθα
2nd p. (————η) τιμᾷ   (——εσθε) τιμᾶσθε
3rd p. (——εται) τιμᾶται   (——ονται) τιμῶνται

Imperfect Tense

1st p. (ἐτιμαόμην) ἐτιμώμην   (——όμεθα) ἐτιμώμεθα
2nd p. (——ου)   ἐτιμῶ   (——εσθε) ἐτιμᾶσθε
3rd p. (——ετο)   ἐτιμᾶτο   (——οντο) ἐτιμῶντο

Imperative Mood
Present Tense

2nd p. (τιμάου) τιμῶ   (——εσθε) τιμᾶσθε
3rd p. (——έσθω) τιμάσθω   (——έσθωσαν) τιμάσθωσαν
     (or -έσθων) or τιμάσθων

Subjunctive Mood
Like the Indicative

Optative Mood
Present Tense

1st p. (τιμαοίμην) τιμῴμην   (——οίμεθα) τιμῴμεθα
2nd p. (——οιο) τιμῷο   (——οισθε) τιμῷσθε
3rd p. (——οιτο) τιμῷτο   (——οιντο) τιμῷντο

Infinitive Mood
Present Tense
(τιμάεσθαι) τιμᾶσθαι

Participle
Masc.   Fem.
(τιμαόμενος) τιμώμενος, (——ομένη) τιμωμένη),
Neut.
(——όμενον) τιμώμενον

CONTRACTED VERBS

Exercise on Contracted Verbs in -αω

Translate and re-translate, as in previous exercises :

(1) Matt. 5, 44 : ἀγαπᾶτε, pres., imperative active of ἀγαπάω ; προσεύχεσθε, pres., imperative of προσεύχομαι (see Deponent Verbs, last Lesson) ; ὑπέρ, for, on behalf of (takes the genitive) ; διωκόντων, gen., plur., pres. partic. of διώκω.

(2) Mark 12, 33 : ἀγαπᾶν, pres. infinitive— the article is not translateable, it indicates the noun character of the infinitive verb, and thus τὸ ἀγαπᾶν are together the subject of ἐστιν ; ἐξ (i.e., ἐκ) " out of " (or "with") ; συνέσεως, genit. of σύνεσις; περισσότερον, a comparative degree, " more." The comparative, which in English is followed by the word "than," is in Greek simply followed by the genitive case. Thus περισσότερον πάντων is not " more of all " but " more than all " ; θυσιῶν, gen., plur. of θυσία.

(3) John 21, 15-16 : ἠρίστησαν, 3rd pers. plur., 1st aorist active, of ἀριστέω ; Σίμων 'Ιωάνου " Simon, son of John " ; the word υἱός, son, was omitted in this phrase ; πλέον, more, a comparative followed by the genitive, i.e., " more than these," see above in (2) ; σύ, note the emphasis on this pronoun ; οἶδας, knowest (an irregular verb).

(4) Matt. 5, 6 : πεινῶντες and διψῶντες (for πεινάοντες and διψάοντες), nom., plur., pres. partic.

141

of πεινάω and διψάω; χορτασθήσονται, 3rd pers. plur., fut. indic., passive, of χορτάζω.

CONTRACTED VERBS WITH -ε- STEMS

These present little difficulty. The -ε- drops out before a long vowel, or vowel combination like -οι- or -ου-. Besides this, -εε- becomes -ει-, and -εο- becomes -ου-. A few tenses will be sufficient to illustrate this. The student should write out the whole of the verb φιλέω in the same way as τιμάω, observing the contractions now mentioned.

(φιλέω), φιλῶ, I love (stem φιλε-)

INDICATIVE MOOD, ACTIVE
Present Tense

1st p.	(φιλέω) φιλῶ	(—έομεν)	φιλοῦμεν
2nd p.	(—έεις) φιλεῖς	(—έετε)	φιλεῖτε
3rd p.	(—έει) φιλεῖ	(—έουσι)	φιλοῦσι

Imperfect Tense

1st p.	(ἐφίλεον) ἐφίλουν	(—έομεν)	ἐφιλοῦμεν
2nd p.	(—εες) ἐφίλεις	(—έετε)	ἐφιλεῖτε
3rd p.	(—εε) ἐφίλει	(—εον)	ἐφίλουν

The remainder of the active and the middle and passive tenses can be formed easily. Here the present participle active contracts as follows: (φιλέων) φιλῶν, (φιλέουσα) φιλοῦσα, (φιλέον) φιλοῦν. The infinitive passive is φιλεῖσθαι (for φιλέεσθαι).

CONTRACTED VERBS IN —οω.

In this third class the following rules should be noted:—

CONTRACTED VERBS

o followed by a long vowel becomes ω.

o followed by a short vowel becomes ου.

o followed by a vowel combination containing ι becomes οι (except in the pres. infin. active, where —οειν becomes —ουν).

(δηλόω) δηλῶ, I manifest (stem δηλο—)

ACTIVE VOICE
INDICATIVE MOOD
Present Tense

	Singular		Plural
1st p.	(δηλόω) δηλῶ		(δηλόομεν) δηλοῦμεν
2nd p.	(—όεις) —οῖς		(—όετε) —-οῦτε
3rd p.	(—όει) —οῖ		(—όουσι) —οῦσι(ν)

Imperfect Tense

This has —ου— throughout: ἐδήλουν (for ἐδήλοον), —ους, —ου, —οῦμεν, etc.

IMPERATIVE MOOD
Present Tense

This has —ου— throughout: δήλου (for δήλοε), δηλούτω, etc.

SUBJUNCTIVE MOOD
Present Tense

1st p.	(δηλόω) δηλῶ		(δηλόωμεν) δηλῶμεν
2nd p.	(—όῃς) —οῖς		(—όητε) —ῶτε
3rd p.	(—όῃ) —οῖ		(—όωσι) —ῶσι(ν)

OPTATIVE MOOD
Present Tense

This has —οι throughout and is like φιλοῖμι.

143

INFINITIVE—*Present :* (δηλόειν) δηλοῦν
PARTICIPLE—*Present :* δηλῶν, δηλοῦσα, δηλοῦν

PASSIVE AND MIDDLE VOICES
INDICATIVE MOOD
Present Tense

δηλοῦμαι, —οῖ, —οῦται (the plur. has —ου— in all persons)

Imperfect Tense

ἐδηλούμην, etc. (—ου— throughout)

IMPERATIVE MOOD
Present Tense

δηλοῦ,—ούσθω, etc. (—ου— throughout)

SUBJUNCTIVE MOOD
Present Tense

δηλῶμαι, δηλοῖ, δηλῶται, etc. (—ω— in plural)

OPTATIVE MOOD
Present Tense

δηλοίμην, etc. (—οι— throughout)

INFINITIVE—*Present :*—δηλοῦσθαι
PARTICIPLE—*Present :*— δηλούμενος, —η, —ον

Note—The future active of the three contracted verbs is τιμήσω, φιλήσω, δηλώσω ; the perfect is τετίμηκα, πεφίληκα, δεδήλωκα ; the first aorist passive, ἐτιμήθην, ἐφιλήθην, ἐδηλώθην ; the perfect middle and passive, τετίμημαι, πεφίλημαι, δεδήλωμαι

*Exercise on Contracted Verbs
in* —εω *and* —οω

CONTRACTED VERBS

Translate and re-translate the following :—

(1) Matt. 10, 37-38 : ὁ φιλῶν is lit. " the one loving " (pres. partic.), i.e., " he that loveth " ; ὑπέρ, above, i.e., " more than " ; θυγατέρα, acc. of θυγάτηρ.

(2) John 21, 16-17 : οἶδας, thou knowest (an irregular verb) : Ποίμαινε, pres. imperative ; τὸ τρίτον, the third time ; ἐλυπήθη, 3rd pers. sing., 1st aorist passive of λυπέω ; εἶπεν, 3rd pers. sing., of an irregular 2nd aor. form of λέγω, he said.

(3) 1 Pet. 1, 11 : ἐραυνῶντες, nom. plur., pres. participle, active, of ἐραυνάω ; εἰς τίνα ἢ ποῖον, "unto what or what sort of " ; ἐδήλου, 3rd pers. sing., imperf., indic., of δηλόω ; προμαρτυρόμενον, nom. sing., neut., pres. partic. of a deponent verb, agreeing with Πνεῦμα (neuter simply in grammatical gender) ; μετὰ ταῦτα, after these things.

(4) Mark 15, 6 : κατά, at ; ἀπέλυεν, 3rd pers. sing., imperf. indic. of ἀπολύω (the imperfect signifying a custom " he used to," etc.—note the augment at the end of the prefixed preposition ἀπε—) ; ἕνα, one ; παρῃτοῦντο, 3rd pers. plur., imperf. indic. of the deponent contracted verb παραιτέομαι (a verb with several meanings, here " to ask ").

Note—Among the contracted verbs, the verb ζάω, I live, which is a little irregular, is important. The present indicative is ζῶ (or ζάω), ζῆς, ζῇ, ζῶμεν, ζῆτε, ζῶσι ; future, ζήσω, or ζήσομαι ; 1st aor. ἔζησα. The present participle ζῶν, ζῶσα, ζῶν, (genitive, ζῶντος, ζώσης, ζῶντος) is very frequent in the New Testament and is found in most of its cases.

Exercise

Translate and re-translate John 6, 51 : καταβάς, 1st aor. partic. of καταβαίνω, "having come down": φάγη, 2nd aor. subjunc. of an irregular verb ἐσθίω, "I eat" (2nd aor., ἔφαγον—formed from another root) ; εἰς τὸν αἰῶνα, lit. "unto the age," signifies "for ever," and must be so translated ; δώσω, I will give (see later).

LESSON XXI

VERBS WITH STEM ENDING IN λ, μ, ν, ρ

Since the consonants λ, μ, ν, ρ are known as liquids, verbs with stems ending in these letters are called LIQUID VERBS. The personal endings are regular throughout, but certain simple changes occur in the preceding syllable or stem ending, as follows :—

(1) While the future tense keeps the verbal stem, which has a short vowel, the present tense stem usually has a long vowel, or, in the case of stems ending in λ, the λ is doubled. Originally the future ended in -σω, as in the regular verb, but the σ dropped.

Thus the stem of the verb αἴρω, I raise, or take up, is ἀρ-, and the future is ἀρῶ. The stem of ἀποκτείνω, I kill, is ἀποκτεν-, and the future is ἀποκτενῶ. Again the stem of ἀγγέλλω (pronounced angellō), I renounce, is ἀγγελ-, and the future is ἀγγελῶ.

Note that the future, active and middle, of liquid verbs is declined like the present of contracted verbs in -εω.

(2) The first aorist, active and middle, omits the σ like the future, but lengthens the vowel

in the preceding syllable by way of compensation.

Thus φαίνω (stem φαν-), I shine, has fut. φανῶ and 1st aor. ἔφηνα; ἀγγέλλω has 1st aor. ἤγγειλα (note the long -ει-).

(3) In the perfect, μ and ν cannot come before κ. One or the other is dropped. So we get κρίνω, I judge, perfect κέκρικα (not κέκρινκα); while, φαίνω has perfect πέφηνα (not πέφηνκα) and μένω has μεμένηκα, lengthening the vowel.

(4) In the perfect passive ν is changed into σ or into μ before the ending -μαι, or else is dropped. Thus φαίνω makes πέφασμαι instead of πέφανμαι; κρίνω makes κέκριμαι instead of κέκρινμαι.

Exercise on Liquid Verbs

Translate and re-translate the following passages :—

(1) Acts 15, 36 : Μετά, after ; εἶπεν, said (an irregular aorist of λέγω) ; Επιστρέψαντες, nom., plur., masc., 1st aorist participle of ἐπιστρέφω, I return (future -ψω) lit. " returning " (the aorist indicating decisive and immediate action); ἐπισκεψώμεθα, 1st pers. plur., 1st aor. subjunc. of the deponent verb ἐπισκέπτομαι, I visit, " let us visit " (the 1st pers. plur. of the subjunc. present and 1st aor. is often used in a hortatory way, "let us," etc.); κατά, throughout; κατηγγείλαμεν, 1st pers. plur., 1st aor., indic. of καταγγέλλω, I

preach (note the position of the augment η, and the long vowel combination ει lengthened from ε after the dropping of the σ in the liquid verb) ; πῶς ἔχουσιν, how they do (lit. "how they have," i.e., "how they are getting on ").

(2) Acts 17, 12-14: γυναικῶν, gen. plur. of γυνή (irregular) ; ἔγνωσαν, 3rd pers. plur., 2nd aor. of γινώσκω, " I know " (irregular) ; κατηγγέλη, 3rd pers. sing., 2nd aor. passive of καταγγέλλω, "was preached," agreeing with its subject λόγος (the 1st aor. passive is κατηγγέλθην—the 2nd aor. is simply an alternative form) ; ἦλθον, 3rd pers. plur., 2nd aor. of ἔρχομαι, I come (see Lesson XIX) ; κἀκεῖ, for καὶ ἐκεῖ, also there ; ἐξαπέστειλαν, 3rd pers. plur., 1st aor. indic. active of ἐξαποστέλλω, " I send away " (note the augment ε after the second preposition ἀπο, and the long ει before the single λ) ; πορεύεσθαι, pres. infin. of πορεύομαι (deponent) ; ἕως, as far as ; ἐπί, to ; ὑπέμειναν, 3rd pers. plur., 1st aor. of ὑπομένω.

(3) Matt. 6, 16-18 : νηστεύητε, pres. subjunc., after the indefinite ὅταν, whenever ; γίνεσθε, 2nd pers. plur., pres. imperat. of γίνομαι (deponent) ; φανῶσιν, 1st aor. subjunc. of φαίνω, I appear (subjunc. of purpose after ὅπως) ; νηστεύων, pres. partic. ; ἄλειψαι, 2nd pers. sing., 1st aor. imperat., middle of ἀλείφω, "anoint for thyself" ; νίψαι, ditto of νίπτω ; ἀποδώσει, shall reward (see later).

THE SECOND CONJUGATION, OR VERBS IN -μι

The student should thoroughly revise the First Conjugation verb before learning the following. The endings of the second conjugation differ from the first only in the present and imperfect tenses, and, in several verbs, in the second aorist active and middle. The other tenses are like those of the First Conjugation, with certain exceptions.

There are two classes, (I) those that double the stem, the reduplication being especially by means of the vowel ι. Thus in δίδωμι, I give, the stem, δο-, is doubled by the prefix δι- ; in τίθημι, I put, the stem, θε-, is doubled by τι- ; in ἵστημι, I place, or stand, the stem, στα-, makes ἱ (for σι) : (II) those that add the syllable -νυ- or -ννυ- to the stem, before the person endings. Thus in δείκνυμι, I show, the stem is δεικ- and -νυ- is inserted before the ending -μι ; in κεράννυμι, I mix (stem κερα-), -ννυ- is inserted.

SECOND CONJUGATION, CLASS I

There are three regular forms, viz., with stems ending in α-, ε-, ω-. The following model paradigms should be memorised, the persons, I, thou, he (she, it), we, you, they, being borne in mind.

SECOND CONJUGATION VERBS

ἵστημι, I stand ; τίθημι, I put ; δίδωμι, I give.

   (stem στα-)   (stem θε-)   (stem δο-)

Note—The following important details must be remembered as to the meanings of the tenses of ἵστημι :—

(1) The present, imperfect, future and 1st aorist of the active voices are transitive, and signify " I cause to stand," " I place," etc.

(2) The perfect and pluperfect are intransitive and are used in a present and imperfect sense, signifying " I stand," " I take my stand," " I was standing." That is to say, these are not to be rendered by " I have stood," " I had stood." These two tenses have a continuous significance and hence we must render by present and imperfect meanings.

(3) The 2nd aorist is also intransitive, and means " I stood."

ACTIVE VOICE

INDICATIVE MOOD

Present Tense

Sing.

ἵστημι	τίθημι	δίδωμι
ἵστης	τίθης	δίδως
ἵστησι(ν)	τίθησι(ν)	δίδωσι(ν)

Plur.

ἵσταμεν	τίθεμεν	δίδομεν
ἵστατε	τίθετε	δίδοτε
ἱστᾶσι(ν)	τιθέασι(ν)	διδόασι(ν)

Imperfect Tense

I was standing, putting, giving, etc.

Sing.

ἵστην	ἐτίθην	ἐδίδουν
ἵστης	ἐτίθεις	ἐδίδους
ἵστη	ἐτίθει	ἐδίδου

Plur.

ἵσταμεν	ἐτίθεμεν	ἐδίδομεν
ἵστατε	ἐτίθετε	ἐδίδοτε
ἵστασαν	ἐτίθεσαν	ἐδίδοσαν

2nd Aorist

I stood

Sing.   No Singular

ἔστην
ἔστης
ἔστη

Plur.

(we gave)

ἔστημεν	ἔθεμεν	ἔδομεν
ἔστητε	ἔθετε	ἔδετε
ἔστησαν	ἔθεσαν	ἔδοσαν

Note—The place of the singular in the *two* last tenses is taken by the 1st aorist ἔδωκα, —κας, —κε.

IMPERATIVE MOOD

Present Tense (continuous action)

Sing.

stand thou   put thou, etc.

ἵστη	τίθει	δίδου
ἱστάτω	τιθέτω	διδότω

SECOND CONJUGATION VERBS

Plur.

ἵστατε	τίθετε	δίδοτε
ἱστάτωσαν	τιθέτωσαν	διδότωσαν

2nd Aorist (immediate action)
(same meaning, but decisive)

Sing.

στῆθι or στα*	θές	δός
στήτω	θέτω	δότω

Plur.

στῆτε	θέτε	δότε
στήτωσαν	θέτωσαν	δότωσαν

Note—στα is used only in compound verbs, as ἀνάστα (Acts 12, 7 : Eph. 5, 14).

SUBJUNCTIVE MOOD
Present Tense
That I, etc., may stand, put, give

Sing.

ἱστῶ	τιθῶ	διδῶ
ἱστῇς	τιθῇς	διδῷς
ἱστῇ	τιθῇ	διδῷ

Plur.

ἱστῶμεν	τιθῶμεν	διδῶμεν
ἱστῆτε	τιθῆτε	διδῶτε
ἱστῶσι(ν)	τιθῶσι(ν)	διδῶσι(ν)

2nd Aorist

στῶ	θῶ	δῶ
etc.	etc.	etc.

(Like the present in each verb)

153

Optative Mood
Present Tense
that I, etc., might stand, put, give

Sing.

ἱσταίην	τιθείην	διδοίην
ἱσταίης	τιθείης	διδοίης
ἱσταίη	τιθείη	διδοίη

Plur.

ἱσταῖμεν	τιθεῖμεν	διδοῖμεν
ἱσταῖτε	τιθεῖτε	διδοῖτε
ἱσταῖεν	τιθεῖεν	διδοῖεν

2nd Aorist
(same meaning, but decisive)

Sing.

σταίην	θείην	δοίην (δῴην)
σταίης	θείης	δοίης (δῴης)
σταίη	θείη	δοίη (δῴη)

Plur.

σταίημεν	θείημεν	δοίημεν
σταίητε	θείητε	δοίητε
σταῖεν	θεῖεν	δοῖεν

Infinitive Mood
to stand, to put, to give

Present	ἱστάναι	τιθέναι	διδόναι
2nd Aor.	στῆναι	θεῖναι	δοῦναι

Participles
Present Tense
standing, putting, giving

ἱστάς, ΄-ᾶσα, -άν τιθείς, -εῖσα, -έν διδούς, -οῦσα, -όν

SECOND CONJUGATION VERBS

2nd Aorist

standing, putting, giving

στάς, -ᾱσα, -άν, θείς, -εῖσα, -έν, δούς, -οῦσα, -όν

Exercise on the above Tenses of the Active Voice of Verbs in μι

Translate and re-translate :—

(1) Luke 6, 8 : ᾔδει, knew (see later) ; εἶπεν, he said ; ἔχοντι, dat., sing., masc., pres. partic. of ἔχω, agreeing with ἀνδρί (dat. of ἀνήρ) ; στῆθι, 2nd aor. imperative ; ἀναστάς, 2nd aor. partic. of ἀνίστημι, I arise, "having arisen" ; ἔστη, 2nd aor. indic. of ἵστημι.

(2) Heb. 3, 12 : βλέπετε, 2nd pers. plur., pres. imperat. ; μή, lest ; ποτε, at any time ; ἔσται, fut. of εἰμί ; ἐν τῷ ἀποστῆναι, lit., " in the to depart from," the verb is the 2nd aor. infin. of ἀφίστημι (a compound of ἀπό and ἵστημι) ; the infinitive is a verbal noun, and is governed by the preposition ἐν, which takes the dative ; hence we must translate by " in departing," the article τῷ not being translated.

(3) Matt. 5, 15 : τιθέασιν, see the pres. indic. of τίθημι ; πᾶσιν, dat. plur. of πᾶς, dative after λάμπει, " it giveth light to."

(4) Luke 12, 25 : μεριμνῶν, nom. sing., masc., pres. partic. of μεριμνάω, " I am anxious " ; δύναται, 3rd pers. sing., pres. indic. of δύναμαι (a deponent verb) ; ἐπί, to ; προσθεῖναι, 2nd aor. infin. of προστίθημι, I put to (πρός and τίθημι).

155

(5) Matt. 7, 7-11 : Αἰτεῖτε, 2nd pers. plur., pres. mperat. of the contracted verb αἰτέω; δοθήσεται, it shall be given (passive of δίδωμι, see later) ; εὑρήσετε, fut. of εὑρίσκω; ἀνοιγήσεται, fut. passive of ἀνοίγω ; πᾶς ὁ αἰτῶν, lit., " everyone the (one) asking," to be rendered " everyone that asketh " ; αἰτήσει, fut., lit., " whom his son shall ask a loaf " ; μή, this is not to be translated, it simply indicates that a negative answer to the question is expected ; ἐπιδώσει, fut. of ἐπιδίδωμι; οἴδατε, know (see later) ; διδόναι, pres. infin.; πόσῳ, how much, dat. of degree, " by how much " ; αἰτοῦσιν, dat., plur., pres. participle, lit., " to the (ones) asking."

LESSON XXII

Note I—The Passive, Indicative, Present of the verb ἵστημι has the meaning of " I am caused to stand," " I am placed," etc., and hence it simply denotes " I stand," etc. Almost the only passive tense used in the New Testament is the 1st aorist.

INDICATIVE MOOD (PASSIVE AND MIDDLE)

I take my stand ; am put ; am given

Sing.

ἵσταμαι	τίθεμαι	δίδομαι
—σαι	—σαι (or τιθῃ)	—σαι
—ται	—ται	—ται

Plur.

—μεθα	—μεθα	—μεθα
—σθε	—σθε	—σθε
—νται	—νται	—νται

Imperfect

I was taking my stand ; was putting ; was giving

Sing.

ἱστάμην	ἐτιθέμην	ἐδιδόμην
—σο	—σο (or ἐτίθου)	—σο (or ἐδίδου
—το	—το	—το

157

Plur.

—μεθα	—μεθα	—μεθα
—σθε	—σθε	—σθε
—ντο	—ντο	—ντο

2nd Aorist (Middle only)

Sing.

	I put	*I gave*
(None)	ἐθέμην	ἐδόμην
	ἔθου	ἔδου
	—ετο	—ετο

Plur.

	—έμεθα	—όμεθα
	—εσθε	—οσθε
	—εντο	—οντο

IMPERATIVE MOOD (PASSIVE AND MIDDLE)
Present Tense
be stood, or stand ; be put, or put ;
be given, or give

Sing.

| ἴστασο, or ἴστω | τίθεσο, or τίθου | δίδοσο, or δίδου |
| ἱστάσθω | τιθέσθω | διδόσθω |

Plur.

| ἴστασθε | τίθεσθε | δίδοσθε |
| ἱστάσθωσαν | τιθέσθωσαν | διδόσθωσαν |

2nd Aorist (Middle only)

Sing.

	put thou	*give thou*
(None)	θοῦ	δοῦ
	θέσθω	δόσθω

Plur.

θέσθε	δόσθε
θέσθωσαν	δόσθωσαν

SUBJUNCTIVE MOOD (PASSIVE AND MIDDLE)
that I might be stood, stand, etc.

Sing.

ἱστῶμαι	τιθῶμαι	διδῶμαι
—ῇ	—ῇ	—ῳ
—ῆται	—ῆται	—ωται

Plur.

—ώμεθα	—ώμεθα	—ώμεθα
—ῆσθε	—ῆσθε	—ῶσθε
—ῶνται	—ῶνται	—ῶνται

2nd Aorist (Middle only)

Sing.

(None)	θῶμαι	δῶμαι
	θῇ	δῷ
	θῆται	δῶται

Plur.

	θώμεθα	δώμεθα
	θῆσθε	δῶσθε
	θῶνται	δῶνται

OPTATIVE MOOD (PASSIVE AND MIDDLE)
Present Tense
that I might be stood, stand, etc.

Sing.

ἱσταίμην	τιθείμην	διδοίμην
—αῖο	—εῖο	—οῖο
—αῖτο	—εῖτο	—οῖτο

Plur.

—αίμεθα	—είμεθα	—οίμεθα
—αῖσθε	—εῖσθε	—οῖσθε
—αῖντο	—εῖντο	—οῖντο

2nd Aorist (Middle only)

Sing.

(None)   θείμην   δοίμην
         θεῖο   δοῖο
Plur.   θεῖτο   δοῖτο

         θείμεθα   δοίμεθα
         θεῖσθε   δοῖσθε
         θεῖντο   δοῖντο

INFINITIVE MOOD (PASSIVE AND MIDDLE)
Present Tense
to be stood, to stand (for oneself), etc.

Ίστασθαι   τίθεσθαι   δίδοσθαι

2nd Aorist (Middle only)
to put for oneself, etc.

(None)   θέσθαι   δόσθαι

PARTICIPLES (PASSIVE AND MIDDLE)
Present
being stood, or standing for oneself, etc.

στάμενος, -η, -ον   τιθέμενος, -η, -ον   διδόμενος, -η, -ον

2nd Aorist (Middle only)
*having been stood or having stood
for oneself, etc.*

(None)   θέμενος, -η, -ον   δόμενος, -η, -ον

Perfect : ἑσταμένος, τεθειμένος,. δεδομένος

SECOND CONJUGATION VERBS

*Exercise on the above Tenses of the Passive and
Middle Voices in Verbs in* -μι.

(1) Jas. 3, 6 : ἐστίν is to be understood in the
first clause ; the verb " to be " is often omitted ;
τῆς, not to be translated, being simply the article
with an abstract noun ; καθίσταται, is set, pres.
ndic. pass. of καθίστημι ; σπιλοῦσα, nom., sing.,
fem., pres. partic. of σπιλέω, lit. " the (one)
defiling " ; φλογιζομένη, pres. partic. pass. ; ὑπό,
by (takes the genit.).

(2) Acts 15, 28: ἔδοξεν, 3rd pers. sing., 1st aor
of δοκέω, " it seemed good"; from μηδέν to
βάρος is *the accusative with the infinitive construction*,
lit. "no greater burden to be put upon, etc."; πλέον,
acc. neut. of πλέων ; ἐπιτίθεσθαι, pres. infin. pass.;
βάρος, acc. case (as βάρος is a neut. noun, μηδέν
is neut. to agree with it) ; πλήν, except (takes
the genit.) ; ἐπάναγκες (here only in New Testament).

(3) 1 Cor. 12, 4-10: τὸ αὐτό (see Lesson V) ;
ὁ ἐνεργῶν, the (one) energising (working in),
i.e., " who worketh in "; πᾶσιν, dat. plur., masc.;
δίδοται, pres. passive (pres. of constant action
" is given ") ; πρὸς, with a view to ; συμφέρον,
acc., neut., pres. partic. of συμφέρω, lit. " profiting "
(i.e., " with a view to the profiting ") ; ᾧ, to
the one (this is the meaning of the relative
pronoun ὅς when followed by ἄλλος, another,
in the next clause) ; κατὰ, according to ;

161

ἑτέρῳ, to another ; ἑνί, dat. of εἷς, " one."

Note—The other tenses, active, passive and middle, of these three verb forms of the 2nd conjugation are formed like those of the 1st conjugation. The indicative mood and the 1st person of the tenses are given ; the other moods and tenses can be formed on the model of λύω. The meanings are regular, save in ἵστημι (see below). Forms not given are not in New Testament.

OTHER TENSES OF VERBS IN -μι

Fut. Active

στήσω	θήσω	δώσω
(I shall cause to stand)	(I shall put)	(I shall give)

1st Aor. Act.

ἔστησα	ἔθηκα	ἔδωκα
(I caused to stand)	(I put)	(I gave)

Perf. Act.

ἔστηκα	τέθεικα	δέδωκα
(I stand)	(I have put)	(I have given)

Pluperf.

ἱστήκειν
or εἱστήκειν ——— ———
(I was standing)

Fut. Passive

σταθήσομαι	τεθήσομαι	δοθήσομαι
(I shall stand)	(I shall be put)	etc.

SECOND CONJUGATION VERBS

1st Aor. Pass.

ἐστάθην	ἐτέθην	ἐδόθην
(I stood)	(I was put)	etc.

Fut. Mid.

στήσομαι	θήσομαι	δώσομαι
(I shall stand)	(I shall put)	etc.

Perf. Mid. or Pass.

———	τέθειμαι	δέδομαι

Note the rough breathings on the perf. and pluperf. of ἵστημι. There are two forms of the perf. partic. act., ἑστηκώς and ἑστώς.

Note that the ending of the 1st aor. active of τίθημι and δίδωμι is -κα and not -σα, as in λύω.

Exercise on the above Tenses of the Three Verbs

Translate and re-translate :—

(1) John 18, 18 : εἱστήκεισαν, pluperf. tense, " they were standing " (not " they had stood," as in ordinary pluperfects) ; πεποιηκότες, nom., plur., masc., perf. partic. act. of ποιέω, "having made " ; ἐθερμαίνοντο, imperf. middle, " were warming themselves " ; ἑστώς, perf. partic., " standing."

(2) John 3, 29 : ὁ ἔχων, the (one) having, i.e., " he that hath " ; ὁ ἑστηκώς, perf. partic. with present meaning, " the (one) standing," i.e., " who standeth " ; ἀκούω takes the genit. ; χαρᾷ, this

dative has the meaning "with joy"; διά, because of; αὕτη ἡ χαρά (see Lesson V, *Personal Pronoun*).

(3) John 19, 41-42 : ἐσταυρώθη, 1st aor. passive of σταυρόω; οὐδέπω οὐδεὶς, lit. "not yet no one," but we must translate by "no one yet"; in Greek two negatives do not, as in English, make a positive, hence the οὐδέπω ("not yet") must be rendered by "yet"; τεθειμένος, perf. partic. passive; ἔθηκαν, 3rd pers. plur., 1st aor. indic.

(4) John 6, 31-39 : ἔφαγον, 3rd pers. plur., 2nd aor. of ἐσθίω (irregular, see later); γεγραμμένον, perf. partic. passive of γράφω; note the different tenses of δίδωμι here, διδούς is pres. part., δός is 2nd aor. imperat.; in verse 35 ὁ ἐρχόμενος (pres. partic. of ἔρχομαι) is "he that cometh" (lit. "the (one) coming"—deponent); οὐ μὴ πεινάσῃ, *this 1st aor. subjunc. with* οὐ μή *is an idiomatic construction used to express a strong negative assurance, "shall by no means," etc. Here again, the two negatives make a strong negative; the construction of* οὐ μή *with 1st aor. subjunc. is very important, and is a curious instance of the use of the 1st aor. with a future meaning;* οὐ μὴ διψήσει (fut. of διψάω) has the same negative assurance, only now the fut. indic. is used, which is according to the usual meaning of that tense; εἶπον, I said (2nd aor. of λέγω, irregular); ἑωράκατε, 2nd pers. plur., perf. indic. of ὁράω (irregular); in ver. 37 note ὃ with the accent, neut. of ὅς,

which ; ἥξει, fut. of ἥκω, I come (a different verb from ἔρχομαι) ; οὐ μὴ ἐκβάλω, another instance of οὐ μή with the fut. (see above, and for ἐκβάλω see on Liquid Verbs, Lesson XXI) ; καταβέβηκα, perf. of καταβαίνω; ποιῶ, subjunc. of purpose after ἵνα ; πέμψαντος, gen., sing., 1st aor. partic. of πέμπω, "of the (one) having sent"; ἀπολέσω, 1st aor. subjunc. of ἀπόλλυμι, "I loose," subjunc. of purpose after ἵνα ; ἐξ αὐτοῦ, of it (ἐξ is for ἐκ, out of) ; ἀναστήσω, fut. of ἀνίστημι.

LESSON XXIII

Special Verbs Belonging to Class 1 of the -μι Conjugation

The following are conjugated like ἵστημι:—

ὀνίνημι, I benefit, once only in New Testament, in Phil. 20, where ὀναίμην is 2nd aor. optat., middle, " may I benefit."

πίμπρημι, I burn, once only in New Testament, Acts 28, 6, where πίμπρασθαι is pres. infin. passive.

φημί, I say; besides this 1st pers., only the following are in New Testament—3rd pers. sing., φησί (ν); 3rd pers. plur., φασί, they say; 3rd pers. sing., imperfect, ἔφη, said he (very frequent).

Deponent Verbs :—

δύναμαι, I am able, -σαι, -ται, etc., as in ἵσταμαι; imper. ἐδυνάμην or ἠδυνάμην; infin. δύνασθαι; partic. δυνάμενος; fut. δυνήσομαι; 1st aor. ἐδυνήθην (or ἠδ . . .)

ἐπίσταμαι, I know, feel sure (only in present tenses in New Testament).

κάθημαι, I sit; 2nd pers. sing. κάθῃ (for καθῆσαι) ; imperf. ἐκαθήμην ; imperat. κάθου ; infin. καθῆσθαι ; partic. καθήμενος.

κεῖμαι, I lie down (this and the preceding verb are really perfects).

ἀφίημι, *I send away, let go, forgive.*

SECOND CONJUGATION VERBS

This is a compound of ἀπό (from) and ἵημι
(I send) only used in New Testament compounded
with a preposition. The forms below (many of
which are irregular) are those most frequent in
New Testament and should be memorised.

Present Indicative

1st p.	ἀφίημι	ἀφίεμεν (or -ομεν)
2nd p.	ἀφεῖς	ἀφίετε
3rd p.	ἀφίησι	ἀφιοῦσι

Imperf. 3rd pers. sing., ἤφιε : note that, contrary
to the rule for the augment (that in a verb
compounded with a preposition the verb itself
receives the augment and not the preposition) the
preposition is augmented here (see Mark 1, 34 ;
11, 16). Pres. imperat. 3rd pers. sing., ἀφιέτω ;
pres. infin. ἀφιέναι; ; fut. indic. ἀφήσω (regular) ;
1st aor. ἄφηκα; 2nd aor. imperat., 2nd pers. sing.,
ἄφες ; 2nd pers. plur. ἄφετε ; 2nd aor. subjunc. ἀφῶ,
etc. ; 2nd aor. partic. ἀφείς, ἀφεῖσα, ἀφέν ; pres.
indic. pass., 3rd pers. plur. ἀφίενται ; perf.
ἀφέωνται; fut. indic. pass. ἀφεθήσομαι (chiefly in
3rd sing. ἀφεθήσεται) ; 1st aor. pass. ἀφέθην.

Exercise on special verbs in Class 1

Translate and re-translate :—

(1) Acts 10, 30-31 : ἔφη (see under φημί) ;
Ἀπὸ, from (takes the genit.) ; μέχρι, until
(takes the genit.) ; ἤμην, an alternative form of
ἦν, I was (imperf. of εἰμί) ; τὴν ἐνάτην, the
ninth (ὥραν "hour" understood), accusative of
time, " at the ninth hour"; προσευχόμενος, pres.

partic. (deponent) : ἔστη (see ἵστημι); ἐνωπιόν, before (takes the genit.); φησίν (see φημί); εἰσηκουσθη, 3rd pers. sing., 1st aor. pass. of εἰσακούω; ἐμνήσθησαν, 3rd pers. plur., 1st aor. pass. of μιμνήσκομαι.

(2) Mark 3, 20-25 : Notice the construction ὥστε μὴ δύνασθαι αὐτούς; *the particle* ὥστε, *so that, is followed by the accusative with the infinitive to express result ;* here αὐτούς is the accusative subject of δύνασθαι, lit., "them to be able," the whole clause being, lit., " so that them not to be able," i.e., " so that they were not able " (cp. ὥστε, etc., in Matt. 8, 24, and in Matt. 13, 32, where ἐλθεῖν is 2nd aor. infin. of ἔρχομαι); ἄρτον is the object of φαγεῖν, which is 2nd aor. infin. of ἐσθίω (irreg.). In ver. 21 οἱ παρ' αὐτοῦ is " the (ones) beside Him," translated freely in A.V., " His friends "; ἀκούσαντες, 1st aor. partic., "having heard "; ἐξῆλθον, 3rd pers. plur. 2nd aor. of ἐξέρχομαι; κρατῆσαι, 1st aor. indic. of κρατέω, to lay hold (decisively) ; ἐξέστη, 2nd aor. indic. of ἐξίστημι, lit., " I stand out," and hence "am insane "; καταβάντες, nom., plur., masc., 2nd aor. partic. of καταβαίνω (a liquid verb, see Lesson XXI) ; ἔλεγον, imperf. " were saying "; ἐν, by ; προσκαλεσάμενος, 1st aor. partic. of the deponent προσκαλέομαι, " I call to myself." In verse 24 ἐφ' is for ἐπί, against ; μερισθῇ, 1st aor. subjunc. pass. of μερίζω; σταθῆναι, 1st aor. infin. pass. of ἵστημι, to stand (not "to

be stood"); στῆναι, 2nd aor. infin. active (here equivalent to the passive in meaning).

(3) Matt. 6, 14-15 : ἀφῆτε, 2nd pers. plur., 2nd aor. subj. of ἀφίημι (the aor. expressing completeness and decision); ἀφήσει, fut. indic.

THE SECOND CLASS OF VERBS IN -μι

Verbs in -νυμι or -ννυμι

Note—Most of these have a second form in the present and imperfect like λύω. Thus δείκνυμι, I show, has another form δεικνύω, and ζώννυμι, I gird, has ζωννύω. All other tenses are formed without the -νυ- and follow the endings of the regular verb.

δείκνυμι, *I show*

Act.	indic.	pres.	δείκνυμι, -νυς, -νυσι (etc. throughout)
		or	δεικνύω, -εις, -ει (like λυω)
,,	,,	imperf.	ἐδείκνυν, -νυς, -νυ, etc.
,,	imperat.	pres.	δείκνυ (or -νυε,), -νύτω, etc.
,,	subj.	,,	δεικνύω, -ῃς, -ῃ, etc.
,,	opt.	,,	δεικνύοιμι, etc.
,,	infin.	,,	δεικνύναι
,,	partic.	,,	δεικνύς, -νῦσα, -νύν (or -νύων, etc.)
Pass. & Mid.	indic.	pres.	δείκνυμαι, etc.
,,	,,	,, imperf.	ἐδεικνύμην, etc.
,,	,,	imperat.	δείκνυσο, etc.
,,	,,	subjunc.	δεικνύωμαι, etc.
,,	,,	opt.	δεικνυοίμην, etc.

Pass. & Mid. infin.   δείκνυσθαι (or -νύεσθαι)
  ,,   ,,   partic.   δεικνύμενος, etc.

Other tenses : Act fut. δείξω ; perf. δέδειχα ;
pass. and mid. perf. δέδειγμαι, etc.

Note that the stem of δείκνυμι ends in a consonant,
δεικ ; the stem of ζώννυμι ends in a vowel, ζω-.
This determines the fut. and 1st aor. endings,
the vowel stems simply taking -σ- ; e.g., ζώσω
ἔζωσα, etc.

VERBS LIKE δείκνυμι

μίγνυμι, I mix ; 1st aor. ἔμιξα ; perf. past
pass. μεμίγμενος.

ἀπόλλυμι, I destroy (ἀπό and ὄλλυμι, the simple verb
not being in New Testament); fut. ἀπολέσω (or
ἀπολῶ) ; 1st aor. ἀπώλεσα (note the ω augment);
perfect, with intransitive meaning " I perish,"
ἀπόλωλα ; partic. ἀπολώλως; pres. partic. mid.
ἀπολλύμενος (plur. " the perishing ") ;. fut. mid.
ἀπολοῦμαι (for -έσομαι, liquid verb) ; 2nd aor.
ἀπωλόμην.

ὀμνύω (or ὄμνυμι), I swear ; 1st aor. ὤμοσα ;
1st aor. infin. ὀμόσαι.

ῥήγνυμι, I tear (also ῥήσσω); fut. ῥήξω; 1st
aor. ἔρρηξα.

ἀμφιέννυμι, I clothe ; perf.· partic. ἠμφιεσμένον
(Matt. 11, 8 : Luke 7, 25).

σβέννυμι, I quench ; fut. σβέσω ; fut. pass.
σβεσθήσομαι.

στρώννυμι, or στρωννύω, I strew, spread; 1st aor. ἔστρωσα; perf. partic. pass. ἐστρωμένος.

For κεράννυμι, I mix, κορέννυμι, I satisfy, ῥώννυμι, I strengthen, see the Lexicon.

Exercise on 2nd Class of Verbs in -μι

Translate and re-translate :—

(1) Acts 2, 22: ἀκούσατε, 1st aor. imperat.; ἀποδεδειγμένον, perf. partic. pass. of ἀποδείκνυμι (see δείκνυμι above); δυνάμεσι, dat. plur. of δύναμις; οἷς, note that this dative plural is attracted to the case of the preceding dative nouns; the strict grammatical construction would be ἅ, acc. plur. as the direct object of ἐποίησεν ("which He did"), but the ἅ becomes οἷς by attraction of the relative pronoun to the preceding noun.

(2) Luke 15, 4: ἑκατὸν, a hundred, is indeclinable; ἀπολέσας, 1st aor. partic. of ἀπόλλυμι (see above), having lost; ἐπὶ, after; ἀπολωλός, acc. sing., neut., perf. partic. (see above); εὕρῃ, 2nd aor. subjunc. of εὑρίσκω.

(3) Heb. 7, 20, 21: καθ' ὅσον, according as; χωρὶς, apart from (takes genit.); οἱ μὲν, they indeed (note this use of the article alone, as a personal pronoun, so ὁ δὲ, but He, in the next clause); γεγονότες, nom., plur., masc., perf. partic. of γίνομαι, I become (see later) with εἰσίν this means "they have become"; μετὰ, with; λέγοντος, gen. sing., masc., pres. partic.; Ὤμοσεν, 1st aor. of ὄμνυμι;; μεταμεληθήσεται, fut. of the deponent verb μεταμέλομαι, "I repent."

(4) Luke 22, 12 : δείξει (see δείκνυμι) ; ἐστρωμένον, perf. partic. of στρώννυμι ; ἑτοιμάσατε, 2nd pers. plur., 1st aor. imperat. of ἑτοιμάζω.

LESSON XXIV

Irregular and Defective Verbs

(I) Some Irregular Futures and 1st Aorists

(*a*) Whereas verbs in -εω make future in -ήσω, the following have -έσω :—ἀρκέω, I suffice; ἐπαινέω, I praise (1st aor. ἐπήνεσα) ; καλέω, I call ; τελέω, I finish; φορέω, I carry. The following makes future and 1st aor. in -ευ- :—πνεώ, I blow, 1st aor. ἔπνευσα. So καίω, I burn, makes καύσω, and κλαίω, I weep, makes κλαύσω.

(*b*) Some verbs in -ίζω make fut. in -ιῶ instead of -ίσω:—ἀφορίζω, I separate; ἐλπίζω, I hope; κομίζω, carry. In these the first aorist resumes the -σ, e.g., ἀφώρισα.

(*c*) Several active verbs have their future in middle form. The following are common and should be memorised :—

ἀκούω,	I hear,	fut.	ἀκούσομαι
ζάω,	I live,	,,	ζήσομαι
λαμβάνω,	I take,	,,	λήψομαι
φεύγω,	I flee,	,,	φεύξομαι
πίνω,	I drink,	,,	πίομαι

(*d*) Some liquid verbs in λ transpose the vowel and the λ in the fut., 1st aor. and perf. passive :—βάλλω, I throw, has fut. pass. βληθήσομαι ; 1st aor. ἐβλήθην ; perf. βέβλημαι : καλέω, I call, has κληθήσομαι, ἐκλήθην, κέκλημαι.

(2) Some Irregular Perfects and Pluperfects

(*a*) Some verbs, instead of reduplicating by the consonant, like λέλυκα, do so by the vowel ε, where the consonant would not sound well : thus ξηραίνω, I wither, has perf. pass. ἐξήραμμαι.

(*b*) Some have a double reduplication, i.e., by both the consonant and a vowel :—ἀκούω, I hear, has perf. ἀκήκοα ; ἔρχομαι, I come, has perf. ἐλήλυθα.

(*c*) Verbs beginning with θ reduplicate by τ, sometimes changing the vowel :—τρέφω, I nourish, makes perf. τέτροφα, and perf. pass. τέθραμμαι ; θραύω, I crush, makes perf. pass. τέθραυσμαι (inserting an σ, see Luke 4, 18).

IRREGULAR AND DEFECTIVE VERBS
(*continued*)

The following list of irregular verbs should be memorised thoroughly. Only the first person singular of the irregular tenses, Indicative, is given ; the other person endings are according to the regular verb. If the following are committed to memory the irregular forms, with which the reader constantly meets in the New Testament, provide no difficulty.

Note—The verbs marked with a dagger are those which derive their forms from different verbal stems. The tenses are thus made up of different verb roots with the same meaning.

IRREGULAR VERBS

Present	Future	1st Aor.	Perfect	2nd Aor.	1st Aor. Passive
ἄγω (lead)	ἄξω	ἦξα	ἦρκα	ἤγαγον	ἤρέθην
† αἱρέω (take)	αἱρήσω			εἷλον	
ἀποθνῄσκω (die)	ἀποθανοῦμαι			ἀπέθανον	
ἀναβαίνω (go up)	ἀναβήσομαι		ἀναβέβηκα	ἀνέβην	
γιγνώσκω (know)	γνώσομαι		ἔγνωκα	ἔγνων	ἐγνώσθην
γίνομαι (become) or	γενήσομαι		γέγονα passive γεγένημαι	ἐγενόμην	ἐγενήθην
γίγνομαι					
ἐγείρω (arouse)	ἐγερῶ	ἤγειρα	ἐγήγερκα		ἠγέρθην
† ἔρχομαι (come)	ἐλεύσομαι		ἐλήλυθα	ἦλθον	
† ἐσθίω (eat)	φάγομαι			ἔφαγον	
ἔχω (have)	ἕξω		ἔσχηκα	ἔσχον	
λαμβάνω (receive)	λή(μ)ψομαι		εἴληφα passive εἴλημμαι	ἔλαβον	ἐλήφθην

175

PRINCIPAL PARTS OF IRREGULAR VERBS—(Continued)

Present	Future	1st Aor.	Perfect	2nd Aor.	1st Aor. Passive
† λέγω (say)	λέξω or ἐρῶ	ἔλεξα	passive λέλεγμαι εἴρηκα εἴρημαι	εἶπον	ἐλέχθην or ἐρρέθην or ἐρρήθην
μανθάνω (learn)	μαθήσομαι		μεμάθηκα	ἔμαθον	
† ὁράω (see)	ὄψομαι		ἑώρακα	* εἶδον	ὤφθην
πάσχω (suffer)			πέπονθα	ἔπαθον	
πίπτω (fall)	πεσοῦμαι		πέπτωκα	ἔπεσον	
† τρέχω (run)	δραμοῦμαι			ἔδραμον	
τυγχάνω (happen)	τεύξομαι			ἔτυχον	
† φέρω (bear)	οἴσω	ἤνεγκα	ἐνήνοχα	ἤνεγκον	ἠνέχθην

176

* *Note*—οἶδα, I know, is a perfect with a present meaning; it is connected with εἶδον, I saw; the pluperfect is ᾔδειν, I knew; the 2nd aorist infin. is ἰδεῖν and the 2nd perfect infin. εἰδέναι.

IRREGULAR VERBS

Exercise on Irregular Verbs

Translate and re-translate :—

(1) John 18, 21, 22 : τί, why ? ; ἐρωτᾷς, 2nd pers. sing., pres. indic. of ἐρωτάω; ἐρώτησον, 1st aor. imperat. ; ἀκηκοότας, acc., plur., masc. of ἀκηκοώς, -υῖα, -ός (gen. -οοτος), perf. partic. of ἀκούω (for the declension of the participle see Lesson X) ; τί, what ; οἴδασιν, 3rd pers. plur. (see note at foot of above list) ; εἶπον (see λέγω, above) ; note the emphatic position of ἐγώ. In ver. 22 note αὐτοῦ εἰπόντος ; *these genitives (i.e., a pronoun or noun, with the participle of a verb each in the genitive case) form what is known as the genitive absolute construction ; it cannot be put literally in English ; the actual English equivalent is " he having said " ; it is best rendered by " when he had said " ; this construction is sometimes used when the main sentence has a different subject (here* εἷς, *one) ;* παρεστηκώς, perf. partic. of παρίστημι, I stand by (" one standing by of the attendants ") ; ἔδωκεν, 1st aor. (" gave ") ; εἰπών, 2nd aor. partic. of λέγω (" saying ") ; ἀποκρίνῃ, 2nd pers. sing., pres. indic. (takes the dative).

(2) John 6, 1, 2 : μετὰ, after ; ἀπῆλθεν, 2nd aor. of ἀπέρχομαι (see list) ; ἠκολούθει, 3rd pers. sing., imperf. of ἀκολουθέω (takes dat.) ; ἑώρων, 3rd pers. plur., imperf. of ὁράω ; ἐπὶ, upon (with gen.) ; ἀσθενούντων, gen., plur., pres. partic. of ἀσθενέω.

177

(3) Mark 6, 27, 28 : ἀποστείλας, 1st aor. partic. of ἀποστέλλω ; ἐπέταξεν, 3rd pers. sing., 1st aor. of ἐπιτάσσω ; ἐνέγκαι, 1st aor. infin. of φέρω (see list) ; ἀπελθών, 2nd aor. partic. of ἀπέρχομαι ; ἀπεκεφάλισεν, 1st aor. of ἀποκεφαλίζω ; ἤνεγκεν (see φέρω).

(4) Matt. 26, 51 : τῶν μετὰ, of the (ones) with ; ἐκτείνας, 1st aor. partic. of ἐκτείνω, " having stretched out " ; ἀπέσπασεν, 1st aor. of ἀποσπάω ; πατάξας, 1st aor. partic. of πατάσσω ; ἀφεῖλεν, 2nd aor. of ἀφαιρέω (see αἱρεω).

(5) John 5, 43 : ἐλήλυθα (see ἔρχομαι, above) ; ἔλθῃ, 2nd aor. subjunc. of the same ; τῷ ἰδίῳ, his own ; λήμψεσθε, fut. of λάμβανω.

(6) 1 Cor. 10, 13 : εἴληφεν, 3rd pers. sing., perf. of λαμβάνω ; εἰ μὴ, except (lit. " if not "). In the next sentence ἐστί is purposely omitted ; ἐάσει, fut. of ἐάω ; πειρασθῆναι, 1st aor. infin. pass. of πειράζω ; τοῦ δύνασθαι, *this construction of the genit. of the article with the infinitive is used to signify purpose*, lit., " (in order to) the being able " ; ὑπενεγκεῖν, 2nd aor. infin. of ὑποφέρω (see above).

(7) Luke 22, 13 : ἀπελθόντες, 2nd aor. partic. of ἀπέρχομαι, " having gone away " ; εὗρον, 3rd pers. plur., 2nd aor. indic. of εὑρίσκω ; εἰρήκει, 3rd pers. sing., plupf. of λέγω, " He had said " ; ἡτοίμασαν, 1st aor. indic. of ἑτοιμάζω.

DEFECTIVE VERBS

IMPERSONAL VERBS

These are used only in the 3rd pers. sing., and in English are translated with the pronoun " it."

The chief impersonal verbs are :—

δεῖ, it is necessary, one ought ; imperf. ἔδει ; subjunc. δέη; ; infin. δεῖν.

δοκεῖ, it seems (from δοκέω).

μέλει, it is a care.

πρέπει, it becomes ; imperf. ἔπρεπε; ; pres. partic. πρέπον, becoming.

χρή, it is expedient, fitting (only in Jas. 3, 10).

Exercise on Impersonal Verbs

Translate and re-translate :—

(1) John 3, 6, 7 : γεγεννημένον, nom., sing., neut., perf. partic. pass. of γεννάω. With the article, this, lit., is " the (thing) having been born," i.e., " that which has been born " ; θαυμάσῃς, 2nd pers. sing., 1st aor. subjunc. of θαυμαζω ; *this tense of the subjunc. with* μή *is used to express a negative command and this is a substitute for the imperative mood*—" do not marvel " ; Δεῖ, it is necessary, is followed by the accusative with the infinitive construction, ὑμᾶς (the accusative) with γεννηθῆναι, 1st aor. infin. passive of γεννάω, lit. " you to be born " ; accordingly the whole phrase " it is necessary you to be born " is to be rendered by " ye must be born." See the same construction in verse 30, " it is necessary Him to increase,

but me decrease" (ἐλαττοῦσθαι, contracted for —όεσθαι, is pres. infin. of ἐλαττόμαι). See again 4, 4, where ἔδει is imperfect, "it was necessary"; διέρχεσθαι, to go through (διά and ἔρχομαι compounded), "it was necessary Him to go through" is "He must needs go through."

(2) Tit. 1, 7-9 : this accus. with the infin. after δεῖ should be clear, and the rest of the verse can be translated with the help of the Lexicon ; note that αὐθάδη is accus., sing., masc. of αὐθάδης, -ης, -ες (see ἀληθής, Lesson X) ; ἀντεχόμενον is pres. partic. of the deponent verb ἀντέχομαι (it takes the genit.) ; καί . . . καί, both . . . and ; ἀντιλέγοντας, acc., plur., pres. partic.

(3) Matt. 17, 25 : ἐλθόντα, acc., sing., 2nd aor. partic. of ἔρχομαι, agreeing with αὐτόν, "him coming . . . Jesus anticipated" (προέφθασεν, 1st aor. of προφθάνω, rendered "prevented" in A.V. and "spake first" in R.V.) ; τί σοι δοκεῖ, what seems it to thee ? (impersonal).

LESSON XXV

NOTES ON THE CASES

THE GENITIVE

(1) The genitive is used (*a*) *with several verbs expressive of sense* or *mental affections*, e.g., ἀκούω, I hear; γεύομαι, I taste; θιγγάνω, I touch; ἐπιθυμέω, I desire; μνημονεύω, I remember; λανθάνω, I forget; (*b*) *with verbs of accusing, and condemning, etc.*, whether of the person accused or of the charge. See, e.g., ἐγκαλέω in Acts 19, 40, and κατηγορέω in John 5, 45 ; (*c*) *with verbs and adjectives of filling, lacking, etc.*, e.g., ἐμπίπλημι in Luke 1, 53, γεμίζω in John 2, 7, ὑστερέω in Rom. 3, 23, and λείπω in Jas. 1, 5 ; (*d*) *with verbs of separation, difference, hindrance*, e.g., μεθίστημι in Luke 16, 4, κωλύω in Acts 27, 43, παύω in 1 Pet. 4, 1, ἀπαλλοτριοῦμαι in Eph. 2, 12, ἀστοχέω in 1 Tim. 1, 6, διαφέρω in 1 Cor. 15, 41, and in Matt. 10, 31, where the meaning is " to be superior " ; (*e*) *with verbs of ruling*, e.g., ἄρχειν, etc., in Mark 10, 42.

(2) For the genitive after adjectives in the *comparative degree* see later.

(3) *Adverbs of time* take the genitive, e.g., ὀψέ, late (Matt. 28, 1), λίαν πρωΐ, very early,

τῆς μιᾶς σαββάτων, an idiom for " the first day of the week " (Mark 16, 2) ; ἅπαξ, once (Heb. 9, 7).

(4) The following *genitive phrases* are used instead of prepositions with a noun : νυκτός, by night (Matt. 2, 14) ; ἡμέρας, by day (Luke 18, 7) ; τοῦ λοιποῦ, for the rest (Gal. 6, 17) ; ποίας (ὁδοῦ), by what (way) (Luke 5, 19).

(5) The *objective genitive* expresses the object of a feeling or action, and must be distinguished from the ordinary subjective genitive expressing possession. Thus προσευχῇ τοῦ Θεοῦ in Luke 6, 12, is " prayer to God " (the preceding article is not to be translated) ; in Rom. 10, 2, ζῆλον Θεοῦ is " zeal towards God " ; in 2 Cor. 10, 5, τοῦ Χριστοῦ is " to Christ " ; so with εἰδώλου in 1 Cor. 8, 7 ; and τοῦ Υἱοῦ in Gal. 2, 20, " in the Son."

(6) The genitive is used in expressing *price, penalty, equivalent, etc.*, ἀσσαρίου in Matt. 10, 29, is " for a farthing " ; cp. τοσούτου, for so much (Acts 5, 8), and δηναρίου, for a penny (Rev. 6, 6).

(7) *The genitive absolute.* The genitive of a noun in agreement with a participle is frequently used in a subordinate sentence without being dependent on any other words, and the genitive refers to some other person or thing than the subject of the principal sentence. In translation this construction is rendered in various ways, e.g., Matt. 17, 9, καταβαινόντων αὐτῶν is, lit., " they descending (from the mountain)," i.e.,

" as they were coming down, etc." The principal
sentence has another subject, viz., ὁ Ἰησοῦς.
The construction is called "absolute," because
it is disconnected from the main sentence. Thus,
again, in Matt. 9, 33, ἐκβληθέντος τοῦ δαιμονίου is
"the demon having being cast out" (gen. of
1st aor. pass. of ἐκβάλλω), and the main sentence
is ἐλάλησεν ὁ κωφός, the dumb man spake.

Exercise

Translate and re-translate :—

(1) Acts 22, 17 : ἐγένετο, it came to pass;
προσευχομένου μου, gen. absolute, "while I was
praying"; γενέσθαι με, acc. with the infin., lit.,
" me to become," i.e., " that I became " or " that
I fell "; so ἰδεῖν, lit., "(me) to see," i.e., " that
I saw." This acc. with infin. construction follows
the impersonal verb " it came to pass " (see later).

(2) Acts 21, 31 : Ζητούντων is the gen. absolute
with the pronoun αὐτῶν not expressed but understood, lit., "(they) seeking (to kill him)," i.e., " as
they were seeking to kill him "; ἀνέβη, 2nd aor.
of ἀναβαίνω; συνχύννεται is present tense but in
English must be rendered by the past, " was in an
uproar " (for this construction see p. 211).

(3) Luke 12, 36 : ἐλθόντος and κρούσαντος are
gen. absolute participles agreeing with αὐτοῦ,
understood, lit. " he coming and knocking ";
ἀνοίξωσιν, 1st aor. subjunc. of ἀνοίγω, subjunc. of
purpose after ἵνα.

o 183

(4) Matt. 2, 13: Note the opening gen. absolute phrase, lit., "they having departed"; ἐγερθείς, nom., sing., masc., 1st aor. partic. pass. of ἐγείρω; παράλαβε, 2nd aor. imperat. of παραλαμβάνω; εἴπω, 2nd aor. subjunc. of λέγω (the ἄν expresses indefiniteness, but is not to be translated); τοῦ ἀπολέσαι, 1st aor. infin. of ἀπόλλυμι, with the article, a phrase of purpose, " to destroy," the infin. being a noun in the genitive case, gen. of intention.

THE DATIVE

(1) Verbs denoting *intercourse, companionship*, *etc.*, take the dative. See the dative after ἀκολουθέω in Matt. 9, 9 ; after κολλάω in Luke 15, 15 ; after ὁμιλέω in Acts 24, 26.

(2) After the verbs " to be," " to become," the dative often denotes *possession*. Thus in Matt. 18, 12, ἐὰν γένηταί τινι ἀνθρώπῳ is lit. " if there be to any man," i.e., " if any man have."

(3) Verbs denoting *assistance* take the dative. See Matt. 4, 11 (διηκόνουν, " they were ministering αὐτῷ to Him ") ; also 15, 25.

(4) Also verbs expressing *mental affections ;* e.g., ὀργίζομαι, I am angry (Matt. 5, 22); ἀρέσκω, I please (Gal. 1, 10) ; πιστεύω, I believe (Matt. 21, 25) ; πείθομαι and ὑπακούω, I obey (Acts 5, 36-37 ; Rom. 10, 16) ; προσκυνέω, I worship (Matt. 2, 2).

(5) The dative expresses *the mode of an action, or the circumstance attending it.* See, e.g., τῇ προθέσει (Acts 11, 23) ; χάριτι (1 Cor. 10, 30) ; παντὶ τρόπῳ, in every way, etc. (Phil. 1, 18) ; προσευχῇ, with prayer (James 5, 17).

(6) The dative expresses *cause or motive.* See, e.g., τῇ ἀπιστίᾳ, through unbelief, and τῇ πίστει, through faith (Rom. 4, 20).

(7) The dative expresses *instrument.* See, e.g., πυρί, with fire (Matt. 3, 12) ; ἀδικίᾳ, etc., by (all) iniquity, etc. (Rom. 1, 29) ; χάριτι, by grace, (Eph. 2, 5-8) ; ἰδίᾳ δόξῃ καὶ ἀρετῇ, by His own glory and virtue (2 Pet. 1, 3). So χράομαι, I use, takes this dative ; see παρρησίᾳ (2 Cor. 3, 12).

(8) The dative sometimes is used to express *the agent.* Note αὐτῷ, by Him (Luke 23, 15) ; ὑμῖν, by you (2 Cor. 12, 20) ; αὐτοῖς, by them (Luke 24, 35).

(9) The dative expresses *the sphere in which a quality exists.* See τῷ πνεύματι, in spirit (Matt. 5, 3) ; τοῖς ποσίν, in his feet (Acts 14, 8) ; φύσει, in nature (Eph. 2, 3).

(10) The dative is used in some expressions of time, either a period or a point. For the period see ἔτεσι, for (about 450) years (Acts 13, 20) ; for the point see τοῖς γενεσίοις αὐτοῦ, on his birthday (Mark 6, 21) ; τῇ τρίτῃ ἡμέρᾳ, on the third day (Matt. 20, 19).

The Accusative

(1) A verb sometimes takes a noun in the accus. case which is akin to it in meaning, and so the meaning of the verb is extended. This is known as the *cognate accusative*. Thus in Matt. 2, 10, ἐχάρησαν χαράν μεγάλην is, lit., "they rejoiced a great joy," i.e., "they rejoiced exceedingly." So in Luke 2, 8, φυλάσσοντες φυλακάς, "watching watches," is "keeping watch." In Col. 2, 19, τὴν αὔξησιν is "with the increase."

(2) An accusative sometimes defines the verb more closely; this is called *the accusative of closer definition*. It must be rendered in English by a prepositional phrase. Thus in John 6, 10, τὸν ἀριθμόν is "in number"; in Phil. 1, 11, καρπὸν is "with the fruit."

(3) *Relations of time and space* are frequently expressed by the accusative, e.g., Luke 22, 41, λίθου βολήν, a stone's throw; so σταδίους in John 6, 19; in Rev. 3, 3, ποίαν ὥραν, what hour, is acc. of time; see ἔτη, years (acc., plur., neut.) in Luke 15, 29.

(4) The accusative is sometimes *irregular*, some word or phrase being understood to complete the sense. See, e.g., ὁδὸν in Matt. 4, 15; γνώστην in Acts 26, 3; τὸ ἀδύνατον, the impossibility, in Rom. 8, 3.

SYNTAX OF CASES

Exercise

Translate and re-translate :—

(1) 1 Pet. 5, 6-9 : αὐτῷ μέλει, lit., "it-is-a-care to Him" (the verb is impersonal), i.e., "He careth" ; ἀντίστητε, 2nd aor. imperat. of ἀνθίστημι, governing the dative ᾧ ; τὰ αὐτὰ . . . ἐπιτελεῖσθαι, accus. with the infin., after εἰδότες, "knowing the same things to be accomplished " ; τῇ . . . ἀδελφότητι, in the brotherhood (see Rule 9 under the Dative).

(2) James 3, 7-10 : τῇ φύσει, etc., dat. of the agent (see Rule 8) " by human nature."

(3) Col. 2, 16-19 : κρινέτω and καταβραβευέτω are 3rd pers. sing., pres. imperat. ; ἑόρακεν, 3rd pers. sing., perf. indic. of ὁράω.

LESSON XXVI

The Comparison of Adjectives

There are three degrees of comparison—Positive,
Comparative, Superlative.

The regular method of forming the comparative
and superlative degrees is by adding -τερος and
-τατος to the stem of adjectives of the 2nd
declension in -ος, and to the stem of those of the
3rd declension in -ης.

Examples

ἰσχυρός, -ά, -όν, strong (stem ἰσχυρο-);
ἰσχυρότερος, -α, -ον, stronger; ἰσχυρότατος, -η,
-ον, strongest.

ἀληθής, -ής, -ές, true (stem ἀληθεσ-); ἀληθέ-
στερος, -α, -ον, truer; ἀληθέστατος, -η, -ον, truest.

Note—When the last vowel but one of the
adjective is short the final ο of the stem is
lengthened to -ω. Thus σοφός, wise, σοφώτερος,
σοφώτατος; νέος, new, νεώτερος, νεώτατος.

The following form their degrees of comparison
irregularly :—

COMPARISON OF ADJECTIVES

Positive	Comparative	Superlative
ἀγαθός, good	κρείσσων (or -ττων), better	κράτιστος, best
κακός, bad	χείρων, or ἥσσων, or ἥττων, worse	χείριστος, worst
πολύς, much or many	πλείων or πλέων, more	πλεῖστος, most
μικρός, little	μικρότερος or ἐλάσσων, less	ἐλάχιστος, least
μέγας, great	μείζων, greater	μέγιστος, greatest

Note I—These comparatives in -ων are declined like σώφρων (acc. -ονα, gen. -ονος, etc., see Lesson X); μείζων has an alternative acc. sing. μείζω (i.e., besides μείζονα), and alternative nom. and acc. plural forms, masc. and fem. μείζους (instead of μείζονες and -ονας), neut. μείζω (instead of μείζονα).

Note II—Adjectives and adverbs in the comparative degree are followed in one or two ways, either (*a*) by ἤ, than, and a noun or pronoun in the same case as the noun or pronoun with which the adjective agrees, or (*b*) simply by the noun or pronoun in the genitive case without ἤ.

Thus (*a*) John 3, 19, μᾶλλον τὸ σκότος ἤ τὸ φῶς, rather the darkness than the light.

(*b*) John 1, 50: μείζω ("greater things," neut. plur. for μείζονα) τούτων ("than these," gen. of comparison) ὄψῃ ("thou shalt see," fut. of ὁράω).

189

GREEK TESTAMENT GRAMMAR

Exercise on the Comparison of Adjectives

Translate and re-translate :—

(1) John 5, 36 : μείζω, acc., sing., fem. ; τελειώσω, 1st aor. subjunc. after ἵνα ; μαρτυρεῖ, sing. after a neut. plur. subject αὐτὰ τὰ ἔργα, " the very works " ; ἀπέσταλκεν, perf. of ἀποστέλλω.

(2) 1 Cor. 1, 24.

(3) Mark 4, 30-32 : ὁμοιώσωμεν, 1st aor. subjunc. (the deliberative subjunctive, " how are we to liken ") ; θῶμεν, 2nd aor. subjunc. of τίθημι ; σπαρῇ, 3rd pers. sing., 1st aor. subjunc. pass. of σπείρω, " I sow " (a liquid verb, see Lesson XXI) ; ὄν, nom., sing., neut., pres. partic. of εἰμί, " being " ; ὥστε δύνασθαι . . . τὰ πετεινά, *the acc. with the infin. after* ὥστε, *" so that," expresses result*, lit., " so that the birds to be able," i.e., "so that the birds are able " ; κατασκηνοῖν, pres. infin.

(4) Heb. 1, 4 : τοσούτῳ, by so much (dat. of degree) ; γενόμενος, 2nd aor. partic. of γίνομαι ; ὅσῳ, by how much ; παρ' αὐτούς, in-comparison-with them."

(5) Matt. 12, 45 : εἰσελθόντα, nom., plur., neut., 2nd aor. partic. of εἰσέρχομαι, " having entered " (note the verb in the sing. following) ; τὰ ἔσχατα, the last things, i.e., " the last state " ; with this the neut. plur. χείρονα agrees.

LESSON XXVII

Adverbs

Adverbs are formed from adjectives by changing the ν of the gen. plur. masc. to ς. Thus the gen. plur. of ἀληθής, true, is ἀληθῶν, and the adverb is ἀληθῶς, truly, verily.

The comparative and superlative degrees of adverbs are formed by using the neut. sing. of the comparative degree of the adjective and the neut. plur. of the superlative of the adjective respectively.

Thus ταχέως is " quickly "; τάχιον, more quickly; τάχιστα, most quickly (Acts 17, 15). Note ὡς with the superlative is idiomatic—ὡς τάχιστα is " as quickly as possible," lit., " as most quickly."

The comparative adverb περισσοτέρως, more abundantly, is formed in the same way as in the positive degree, and not by the neut. sing. (2 Cor. 11, 23).

Note the adverb ὄντως, truly; it is formed from the pres. partic. of εἰμί.

The following irregular comparisons should be memorised :—

Positive	Comparative	Superlative
εὖ, well	βέλτιον or κρείσσον, better	
καλῶς, well	κάλλιον, better	
κακῶς, badly	ἧσσον (or -ττον), worse	
πολύ, much	μᾶλλον, more πλεῖον or πλέον, more	μάλιστα, most

Forms omitted in the above are not found in the New Testament.

Exercise on Adverbs

Translate and re-translate :—

(1) Heb. 2, 1: δεῖ, impersonal, "it is necessary"; this is followed by the acc. with the infin. ἡμᾶς προσέχειν, lit., "us to give heed," i.e., "that we should give heed"; περισσοτέρως, more abundantly, i.e., "more earnestly"; ἀκουσθεῖσιν, dat., plur., neut., 1st aor. partic. pass. "to the (things) having been heard."

(2) 2 Tim. 1, 18: δῴη, 3rd pers. sing., 2nd aor. subjunc. of δίδωμι, the subjunc. of a wish, "may He give"; εὑρεῖν, 2nd aor. infin. of εὑρίσκω; βέλτιον, lit. "better," the comparative being here equivalent to the superlative "very well."

(3) John 20, 4: ἔτρεχον, imperf.; προέδραμεν, 2nd aor. of προτρέχω, "I run before."

ADVERBS

(4) 1 Thess. 2, 13 : παραλαβόντες, 2nd aor. partic. of παραλαμβάνω ; ἐδέξασθε, 1st aor. of δέχομαι.

Note to Students—The Lesson on " Some Additional Rules of Syntax " may be taken next, the intervening Lessons being postponed.

LESSON XXVIII

Prepositions (Part I)

The special significance of the cases in nouns, etc., was pointed out in Lesson II. The relations broadly stated there, and a variety of others, are expressed also by means of prepositions. Thus, while the accusative itself chiefly signifies motion towards, this relation may be expressed by such a preposition as πρός, with the accusative of the following noun. Again, one of the meanings of the genitive case is motion from, and this is likewise conveyed by ἀπό, with that case of the following noun. The dative may signify rest in a place, or the instrument of an action, etc., and each of these is expressed, e.g., by ἐν with the dative of the noun ; a useful example of ἐν in this way is ἐν μαχαίρᾳ, with a sword (Luke 22, 49).

Sometimes the use of the preposition is merely emphatic. The case of the noun alone would have expressed the same meaning, but with less force. In most instances, however, the preposition denotes a relation which the noun itself would be insufficient to indicate.

Some prepositions govern one case only ; others govern two cases with different meanings ; a few are used with three cases, the meanings differing in each case.

SYNTAX OF PREPOSITIONS

Again, the same preposition may have a considerable variety of meanings, and the actual sense must be gathered largely from the context.

Certain prepositions are closely allied in some of their meanings. They express much the same relationship but from different points of view. In English, for instance, we use the prepositions " by " and " through " to signify the same transaction, yet there is a real distinction. We say that something is done by a person, or through him. These prepositions are not, however, synonymous or interchangeable, and in Greek it is specially necessary to observe the distinction.

It is important for the student to become thoroughly acquainted with all the prepositions. The list should be committed to memory.

(a) PREPOSITIONS GOVERNING ONE CASE ONLY

(1) *Those used with the accusative only*

ἀνά and εἰς

ἀνά, up. This is frequently compounded with verbs. Separately with a noun it has a special meaning, as ἀνὰ μέσον, in the midst of (Mark 7, 31 ; Rev. 7, 17) ; ἀνὰ μέρος, by turn (1 Cor. 14, 27) ; with numerals, ἀνὰ δύο, two by two (Luke 10, 1) ; with measures, signifying " apiece," ἀνὰ δηνάριον, a denarius, apiece (Matt. 20, 9, 10) ; ἀνὰ μετρητάς, measures a- piece (John 2, 6) ; in Rev. 21, 21 ἀνὰ εἰς ἕκαστος is " each one separately."

εἰς, to, unto, into, towards. This is used (*a*) of place, and the proper meaning is to be gathered from the context ; (*b*) of persons, " towards " or " with reference to," as in Rom. 12, 16; Acts 2, 25, or " over against," as in Luke 12, 10 ; εἰς Χριστόν is " unto Christ " (Rom. 6, 3) ; (*c*) "of purpose," " with a view to," " in order to," " for " ; εἰς τὸ σταυρωθῆναι, lit. " unto the to-be-crucified," i.e., " in order to be crucified" (Matt. 26, 2) ; cp. 1 Cor. 11, 24 ; (*d*) to express equivalence (Rom. 4, 3) ; (*e*) with the meaning of ἐν, e.g., εἰς τὸν ἀγρόν, in the field (Mark 13, 16), cp. Acts 8, 40 : 21, 13.

(2) *Those used with the genitive only*

ἀντί, ἀπό, ἐκ, πρό

ἀντί, over against, instead of, for ; the idea is that of an equivalent, often with the sense of opposition. Note the phrase ἀνθ᾽ ὧν, lit. " in return for which things," i.e., " because," Luke 1, 20 : 12, 3 : 19, 44 ; 2 Thess. 2, 10.

ἀπό, from (from the exterior) ; sometimes this is equivalent to " on account of," as in Matt. 18, 7.

Note the phrases with adverbs ἀπὸ τότε, from then (Matt. 4, 17) ; ἀπ᾽ ἄρτι, henceforth, (Matt. 23, 39) ; ἀπὸ τοῦ νῦν, from now (Luke 1, 48, etc.), and others.

ἐκ or ἐξ, from (the interior) ; this is used of place, origin, source, cause. Note the use signifying belonging to a class, e.g., ὁ ὢν ἐκ τῆς ἀληθείας, he who is of the truth, cp. Rom. 2, 8 : 4, 12-14 ;

Gal. 3, 9 ; also those referring to time, e.g., ἐκ τούτου, from this time (John 6, 66) ; ἐξ ἐτῶν ὀκτώ, for eight years (Acts 9, 33).

πρό, before, used of time or place, and in the phrase πρὸ πάντων, before all things, of superiority.

PREPOSITIONS USED WITH THE DATIVE ONLY
ἐν and σύν

ἐν, in, used of time or place. Like ἐκ, this may be used to denote " on," as in ἐν τῷ θρόνῳ μου (Rev. 3, 21) ; cp. Heb. 1, 3. It signifies " among " in Matt. 2, 6 ; Acts 2, 29 ; 1 Pet. 5, 1-2, and with numbers, e.g., ἐν δέκα χιλιάσιν, among ten thousands.

It is also used to denote *accompaniment*, or even *instrument*, 1 Tim. 1, 18; Heb. 9, 25; Eph. 6, 2; Luke 22, 49; Matt. 5, 34 : 9, 34.

Note its use with a noun adverbially, e.g., ἐν τάχει, speedily (Rev. 1, 1).

Also its use with the infinitive as a noun, where it signifies " while." Thus in Matt. 13, 4, ἐν τῷ σπείρειν αὐτόν, lit., " in the him to sow," i.e., " while he was sowing " (an acc. with the infin., both with the article, and all governed by the preposition). With relative pronouns it denotes " whilst " ; see ἐν ᾧ in Mark 2, 19 ; so ἐν οἷς in Luke 12, 1 is " whilst."

σύν, together with. Occasionally this denotes " besides." Thus in Luke 24, 21, ἀλλά γε

καί (lit. " but indeed also," i.e., " moreover ")
σὺν πᾶσι τούτοις, beside all this (lit. " these
things ").

Exercise

Translate and re-translate :—

(1) 2 Pet. 1, 5-8 : αὐτὸ τοῦτο, this phrase,
lit., " itself this," is an adverbial accusative and
must be translated " for this very (cause) " ;
παρεισενέγκαντες, nom., plur., 1st aor. partic. of
παρεισφέρω (see φέρω in list of irregular verbs,
Lesson XXIV) ; καθίστησιν, note this 3rd pers.
sing. after the neut. plur. subject ταῦτα.

(2) Eph. 1, 3-8 : ἐξελέξατο, 1st aor. mid. of
ἐκλέγω ; ἧς in verse 6 is an example of the
attraction from the acc., as the object of the
following verb, to the genitive of the preceding
word but one, χάριτος : we must not translate by
" of which " but by " which " (the R.V. text is
right, not the margin) ; " freely-bestowed " is all
one word.

LESSON XXIX

PREPOSITIONS (PART II)

PREPOSITIONS USED WITH THE ACCUSATIVE AND
GENITIVE CASES

διά, κατά, μετά, περί, ὑπέρ, ὑπό

διά with the accusative means " on account of,"
" because of."

διά with the genitive has three chief meanings :—

(1) of *place*, signifying " through " (John 4, 4 ;
1 Cor. 13, 12).

(2) of *instrument*, signifying " by means of,"
" through " (2 Thess. 2, 2).

(3) of *time*, signifying (*a*) " during " (Heb.
2, 15) ; διὰ νυκτός is " by night " (i.e., during,
without reference to a particular time), Acts
5, 19 ; (*b*) " after " (Matt. 26, 61).

κατά with the accusative means :—

(1) of *place*, either (*a*) " throughout " (Luke
8, 39), or (*b*) " before " (Luke 2, 31), or distributively, e.g., διώδευεν (" He was journeying "—
impf. of διοδεύω) κατὰ πόλιν, from city to city
(Luke 8, 1).

(2) of *time*, (*a*) " in " or " at " (Matt. 1, 20),
(*b*) distributively, κατ᾽ ἔτος, year by year

(Luke 2, 41), καθ' ἡμέραν, daily (Matt. 26, 55) ; καθ' εἷς (or καθεῖς), one by one (John 8, 9).

(3) of *comparison*, " according to." Note κατὰ πίστιν, according to faith (Heb. 11, 13) ; also the idioms κατ' ἰδίαν, alone (Matt. 14, 13), καθ' ἑαυτόν, by himself (Acts 28, 16).

κατά with the genitive means either (*a*) " down " (Matt. 8, 32) or (*b*) " against " (Mark 11, 25) or (*c*) " throughout " (Luke 4, 14).

μετά with the accusative means " after " (Matt. 26, 2) ; in Luke 22, 20, μετὰ τὸ δειπνῆσαι is " after supper " (the verb in the aor. infin. being equivalent to a noun).

μετά with the genitive means " with " (Matt. 1, 23).

περί with the accusative means (1) of *place*, " around " (Matt. 8, 18) ; (2) of *time*, " about " (Matt. 20, 3) ; (3) of *an object of thought*, " about " (Luke 10, 40) or " with reference to " (1 Tim. 1, 19).

περί with the genitive means " about " or " concerning " (Acts 8, 12), sometimes almost like ὑπέρ, for (Rom. 8, 3 ; 1 Thess. 5, 25).

ὑπέρ with the accusative means " above " and is used in comparison (Matt. 10, 24) ; note the use after a comparative adjective for the sake of emphasis where the meaning is " than " (Luke 16, 8 ; Heb. 4, 12).

ὑπέρ with the genitive means " on behalf of," " for " (1 Cor. 15, 3 ; 2 Cor. 5, 14-15).

ὑπό with the accusative means "under" (Matt. 5, 15); note the phrase in Acts 5, 21, ὑπὸ τὸν ὄρθρον, under (i.e., close upon) the dawn, i.e., very early in the morning.

ὑπό with the genitive means "by" (Matt. 4, 1).

PREPOSITIONS USED WITH THE ACCUSATIVE, GENITIVE AND DATIVE

ἐπί, παρά, πρός

ἐπί with the accusative has the following meanings :—

(1) of *place*, "upon," with the idea of motion (Matt. 5, 15); note the use after the verb "to hope" (1 Tim. 5, 5, and ch. 4, 10, where the preposition is used with the dative, "upon" of rest rather than motion—see below).

(2) of *authority*, "over" (Luke 1, 33).

(3) of *intention*, "for" or "against" (Matt. 3, 7 : 26, 55).

(4) of *direction*, "towards," "with regard to" (Luke 6, 35 ; Mark 9, 12).

(5) of *quantity*, "up to," e.g., ἐπὶ πλεῖον, to a further point, i.e., any further (Acts 4, 17). Note the phrase ἐφ᾽ ὅσον, inasmuch as, also used of time, "as long as" (Matt. 9, 15).

(6) of *time*, "during," "for" (Luke 10, 35 : 18, 4). Note the phrase ἐπὶ τὸ αὐτό, at the same place, or at the same time, i.e., together (Luke 17, 35 ; Acts 2, 1, etc.).

ἐπί with the genitive has the following meanings :—

(1) of *place*, "upon" (Matt. 6, 10); so figuratively (John 6, 2) ; or "before" (1 Tim. 5, 19), or "on the basis of," e.g., ἐπ' ἀληθείας, in truth (Mark 12, 14); cp. 2 Cor. 13, 1.

(2) of *authority*, "over" (Acts 6, 3).

(3) of *time*, "in the time of" (Luke 3, 2 ; Rom. 1, 10 ; Heb. 1, 2).

ἐπί with the dative has the following meanings :—

(1) of *place*, "upon," with rest implied (Luke 21, 6).

(2) of *superintendence*, "over" (Luke 12, 44).

(3) of *condition, ground, etc.*, "on" or "at" (Matt. 4, 4 ; Mark 9, 37 ; Acts 11, 19). Note the phrase ἐφ' ᾧ, on condition that, wherefore, because (Rom. 5, 12, etc.).

(4) of *quantity*, "beside," "in addition to" (Luke 3, 20).

παρά with the accusative has the following meanings :—

(1) of *place*, "by," "near" (Matt. 13, 4 ; Acts 10, 6).

(2) of *contradistinction*, "contrary to," "rather than" (Rom. 1, 25-26 : 4, 18).

(3) of *comparison*, "above," "than" (Luke 13, 2 ; Heb. 9, 23).

Note the phrase παρὰ τοῦτο, therefore, in 1 Cor. 12, 15-16, where the idea is that of consequence through comparison.

παρά with the genitive means " from " (beside and proceeding from) ; it is used of persons (Matt. 2, 4 ; John 16, 27). Note the phrase οἱ παρ᾽ αὐτοῦ, lit., " those from Him," i.e., " His friends."

παρά with the dative means " with," whether of *nearness*, as in John 14, 17 ; 19, 25 ; Acts 10, 6 ; or of *estimation* or *ability*, as in Matt. 19, 26 ; Rom. 2, 13. Note the phrase παρ᾽ ἑαυτοῖς, lit., " with yourselves," i.e., " in your own conceits."

πρός with the accusative has the following meanings :—

(1) of *direction*, " to " (1 Cor. 13, 12) : δεῦτε πρός με is " hither to me " (Matt. 11, 28).

(2) of *company* with the thought of attitude towards, " with " (John 1, 1 ; Matt. 13, 56).

(3) of *mental direction*, either " towards " or " against " (Luke 23, 12 ; Acts 6, 1). Note the meaning " in regard to " in Heb. 1, 7.

(4) of *estimation*, " in consideration of " (Matt. 19, 8 ; Luke 12, 47 ; Rom. 8, 18).

(5) of *purpose*, " for," " in order to " (Matt. 6, 1 ; 1 Cor. 10, 11).

πρός with the genitive occurs once only in New Testament in Acts 27, 34, where the idea is " belonging to " or " for."

πρός with the dative means " near," " at," or " about " (Luke 19, 37 ; John 20, 12).

Exercise

Translate and re-translate :—

(1) Heb. 9, 24-27 : note κατ' ἐνιαυτὸν, " year by year " (verse 25) ; in verse 26 note the acc. with the infin. αὐτὸν . . . παθεῖν (from πάσχω), after the impersonal ἔδει, it was necessary Him to suffer ; in verse 27 καθ' ὅσον is " according as " (lit., " according to how much ").

(2) Luke 10, 35-37 : note the acc. and infin. after ἐν τῷ . . . , lit., " in the me to come back," where the phrase " me to come back " is a noun clause agreeing with τῷ, the whole governed by ἐν ; δοκεῖ σοι, does it seem to thee ; ἐμπεσόντος, gen. of 2nd aor. partic. of ἐμπίπτω ; μετ' αὐτοῦ, lit., " with him."

LESSON XXX

INTERROGATIVE PARTICLES AND NUMERALS

(a) Sometimes εἰ, if, is used elliptically, i.e., without any preceding clause such as " Tell us " or " Say." Thus in Matt. 12, 10 εἰ ἔξεστι is " is it lawful ? " In Acts 19, 2 εἰ . . . ἐλάβετε is " did ye receive " (for " tell me if ye received "). See also Acts 7, 1 : 21, 37 : 22, 25.

(b) ἤ is occasionally used to introduce a question ; in this case, too, a former clause is to be understood. See Rom. 3, 29 : 6, 3 : 7, 1.

(c) ἆρα introduces a question in three places, Luke 18, 8 ; Acts 8, 30 ; Gal. 2, 17. It is not to be translated. It is to be distinguished from ἄρα with the acute accent, which means " then " or " accordingly," as in Gal. 2, 21.

Exercise on the Particles

Translate and re-translate :—

(1) Acts 6, 15 : 7, 1 ; εἰ is not to be translated ; οὕτως ἔχει is, lit., " have thus " (sing. verb after neut. plur. subject), i.e., " have these things thus," is " are these things so ? "

(2) Rom. 6, 3: ὅσοι followed by the 1st pers. plur. of the verb is " as many (of us) as were, etc.,"

i.e., " all we who were . . ."; συνετάφημεν, 1st pers. plur., 2nd aor. indic., passive of συνθάπτω (note the irregular formation and the regular augment after the preposition).

(3) Rom. 7, 1 : γινώσκουσιν, dat., plur., masc., pres. partic. (not 3rd pers. plur., pres. indic.), lit., " to the (ones) knowing," i.e., " to them that know."

(4) Gal. 2, 17 : εὑρέθημεν, 2nd aor. indic. pass.; in the sentence beginning with ἄρα, the verb ἐστί is understood. The verb " to be " is frequently omitted.

NUMERALS

The Cardinal Numerals

The numbers εἷς, one ; δύο, two ; τρεῖς, three ; τέσσαρες, four, are declined as follows :—

	Masc.	Fem.	Neut.
Nom.	εἷς	μία	ἕν
Acc.	ἕνα	μίαν	ἕν
Gen.	ἑνί	μιᾷ	ἑνί

Nom., Acc., Gen., δύο ; Dat., δυσί(ν).

Nom. and Acc., Masc. and Fem., τρεῖς ; Neut., τρία.

Gen. in all three genders, τριῶν.

Dat. ,, ,, ,, ,, τρισί.

Nom. and Acc., Masc. and Fem., τέσσαρες, Neut., —α.

NUMERALS

Gen. in all three genders, τεσσάρων.

Dat. „ „ „ „ τέσσαρσι(ν).

Like εἷς are declined its negative compounds οὐδείς and μηδείς, no one.

The rest of the cardinal numerals in New Testament are to be found in the Lexicon.

The signs for numerals are not numbers but letters with an accent : 1 is α′ ; 2 is β′ ; the letters after θ′ go in tens : ι′ is 20 ; κ′ is 30 ; but this goes only to π′, 80 ; after this the letters go in hundreds : ρ′ is 100 ; χ′ is 600. Thus 666 is χξϛ′ (Rev. 13, 18). ϛ′ is 6 ; ϙ‘ is 90 ; ϡ′ is 900.

THE ORDINAL NUMERALS

For " first " the superlative πρῶτος is used. Succeeding numbers are formed from the stems of their cardinal numbers and are declined like adjectives of the first two declensions—in -ος, etc. Cardinal numbers are sometimes used instead of ordinals in reckoning the days of the week.

DISTRIBUTIVE NUMERALS

These are formed either by repeating the number or by a preposition with the number. Thus, " two and two " is either δύο δύο (Mark 6, 7) or ἀνὰ δύο (Luke 10, 1). " One by one " is εἷς καθ’ εἷς in Mark 14, 19 and John 8, 9.

LESSON XXXI

SOME ADDITIONAL RULES OF SYNTAX

Several rules of Syntax have been noted in the exercises. A few of the most important are given here.

(a) NEGATIVE QUESTIONS

(1) When οὐ is used in a negative question an affirmative reply is expected. See, e.g., 1 Cor. 9, 1.

(2) When μή is used a negative answer is expected, but the μή is not to be translated. Thus μὴ ἀδικία παρὰ τῷ Θεῷ, Is there unrighteousness with God? (Rom. 9, 14). The negative may be brought out in this way, " There is not unrighteousness with God, is there? " But that is not a translation.

(3) μήτι more strongly suggests a negative answer. See Matt. 7, 16 : 26, 22, 25.

(b) SOME USES OF THE SUBJUNCTIVE MOOD

(1) In *exhortations* in the 1st person (the negative is always μή). Thus in John 19, 24, μὴ

σχίσωμεν, " let us not rend," the verb is 1st aor. subjunc. of σχίζω, and λάχωμεν, " let us cast lots," is the 2nd aor. subjunc. of λαγχάνω.

(2) In *prohibitions* the subjunctive aorist is used with μή, as an alternative to the imperative. See ἐνδύσησθε in Matt. 6, 25, and note the imperative μεριμνᾶτε, preceding.

(3) Similarly in *requests*. See εἰσενέγκῃς in Matt. 6, 13, the 1st aor. subjunc. of εἰσφέρω.

(4) In *deliberative questions* or those expressing doubt. In 1 Cor. 11, 22, εἴπω is 2nd aor. subjunc. of λέγω, and ἐπαινέσω is 1st aor. subjunc. of ἐπαινέω.

(5) *Strong denials* take the aorist subjunctive with the double negative οὐ μή. See Matt. 5, 18-20 : 24, 2 : 24, 35 ; Luke 6, 37 ; John 6, 37 : 8, 51 : 10, 28: 13, 8; Heb. 13, 5; where ἀνῶ is 2nd aor. subjunc. of ἀνίημι.

Exercise

Translate and re-translate :—

(1) 1 Cor. 8, 13.

(2) 1 Thess. 4, 15 : φθάσωμεν, 1st aor. subjunc. of φθάνω.

(3) 1 Thess. 5, 6.

(4) Matt. 26, 53-54.

(c) THE OPTATIVE MOOD

(1) This expresses wishes. See, e.g., 1 Thess. 3, 11-12, where all the optatives are 1st aorists. The negative is μή. See, e.g., Mark 11, 14 ; φάγοι is 2nd aor. opt. of ἐσθίω.

(2) With ἄν there is a potential sense, expressing possibility ; ἄν is never translateable. See, e.g., Acts 8, 31.

Exercise

Translate and re-translate :—

(1) Acts 8, 20 : εἴη εἰς ἀπώλειαν is " may it be unto destruction," i.e., " may it perish."

(2) 2 Thess. 3, 5.

(3) Acts 26, 29.

LESSON XXXII

Rules of Syntax (*Continued*)

(*d*) DEPENDENT CLAUSES

Note—Sentences containing dependent clauses consist of a principal clause containing the main subject and its predicate or verb, and one or more subordinate or dependent clauses. These latter may be formed in a variety of ways, as follows :—

(I) Object Clauses. Here the subordinate clause is itself the object of the verb in the principal clause. Thus in Matt. 9, 28, πιστεύετε ὅτι δύναμαι τοῦτο ποιῆσαι the clause from ὅτι to ποιῆσαι is the object of πιστεύετε.

(*a*) If the verb in the principal clause is in the past tense the verb in the dependent clause is usually in the present indicative (sometimes the optative), but must be translated in English by the past tense. Thus in John 11, 13, ἐκεῖνοι δὲ ἔδοξαν ὅτι . . . λέγει is, lit , "but they thought that He is speaking." We must render by " that He was speaking." Cp. John 20, 14 ; Mark 5, 29.

(*b*) Sometimes ὅτι serves to introduce a *quotation :* it is not to be translated in that case. See, e.g., Matt. 7, 23 ; Luke 8, 49.

(c) In *indirect questions* the verb in the object clause is found either in the indicative, or the subjunctive or the optative.

The indicative intimates that the object of inquiry concerns a matter of fact. See, e.g., Luke 23, 6, ἐπηρώτησεν εἰ . . . ἐστι, "he asked if he were . . ." (here also the verb in the dependent clause goes into the present tense) ; cp. Acts 10, 18.

The subjunctive expresses future possibility. See, e.g., Matt. 6, 25, and Luke 19, 48, where ποιήσωσιν is 1st aor. subjunc.

The optative expresses the possibility of what may be thought to exist or to have existed. See, e.g., Luke 1, 29 ; Acts 17, 11 : 17, 27 (εὕροιεν is 2nd aor. opt.). See both indic. and opt. in Acts 21, 33.

(II) CONDITIONAL CLAUSES. The dependent clause begins with " if." There are four kinds of supposition :—

(a) The supposition of a fact. Here the dependent or εἰ clause has the indicative. See, e.g., Matt. 4, 3 ; Rom. 4, 2.

(b) The supposition of a possibility, or uncertainty with the prospect of decision. Here ἐάν (i.e., εἰ ἄν) is used with the subjunctive (rarely εἰ). See, e.g., Matt. 17, 20 ; John 3, 3-5 ; 2 Tim. 2, 5.

(c) The supposition of an uncertainty. Here the optative is used, and always with εἰ. See, e.g., 1 Pet. 3, 14 ; Acts 24, 19.

DEPENDENT CLAUSES

(d) The supposition of an unfulfilled condition. Here the indicative is used with εἰ in the dependent clause, and the main clause takes ἄν. Two tenses are chiefly used in this main clause, the imperfect and the aorist.

When the imperfect is used with ἄν, present time is indicated, e.g., " If this were so (which is not the case), something else would be taking place (but it is not so)." Thus in John 8, 42, Εἰ ὁ Θεὸς Πατήρ ὑμῶν ἦν, ἠγαπᾶτε ἄν ἐμέ, If God were your Father (which is not the case), ye would love Me (but ye do not). Note the imperfect tense with ἄν. See, e.g., Luke 7, 39 ; John 5, 46 ; Heb. 4, 8.

When the aorist is used with ἄν, past time is indicated, e.g., " If this had been so (which was not the case) something else would have occurred (but it did not)." Thus, in 1 Cor. 2, 8, εἰ γὰρ ἔγνωσαν, οὐκ ἄν . . . ἐσταύρωσαν, For if they had known (which was not the case) they would not have crucified . . . (but they did so). See, e.g., John 14, 28 ; Luke 12, 39 (where ἀφῆκεν is 1st aor. of ἀφίημι). Sometimes the pluperfect is used with ἄν. See John 11, 21 : 14, 7.

Exercise on Object and Conditional Clauses

Translate and re-translate :—

(1) Luke 17, 15 : ἰάθη, 1st aor. indic. pass. of ἰάομαι; ; ὑπέστρεψεν, 1st aor. of ὑποστρέφω.

(2) Mark 15, 44 : τέθνηκεν, perf. of θνήσκω ; προσκαλεσάμενος, 1st aor. partic. middle ; ἀπέθανεν, 2nd aor. of ἀποθνήσκω.

213

(3) Heb. 11, 15 : ἐξέβησαν, 1st aor. of ἐκβαίνω
(note the change of κ to ξ before the ε augment) ;
εἶχον, imperf. of ἔχω ; ἀνακάμψαι, 1st aor. infin. of
ἀνακάμπτω.

(4) Mark 13, 20 : ἐκολόβωσεν, 1st aor. of
κολοβόω ; ἐξελέξατο, 1st aor. mid. of ἐκλέγω.

(5) Matt. 23, 30.

(III) FINAL CLAUSES OR CLAUSES OF PURPOSE.
These are introduced either by ἵνα, to the end
that (with stress on the result) or ὅπως (with
stress on the method) or μή (signifying " lest " or
" that . . . not "). See also p. 88.

(a) The verb in the dependent clause is usually in
the subjunctive. See, e.g., Matt. 2, 8 : 6, 16 ;
Luke 6, 34. The negative is always μή. See, e.g.,
Matt. 18, 10 ; Heb. 12, 15, 16. After verbs of
fearing μή is rendered by " lest " or " that."
See, e.g., 2 Cor. 12, 20-21.

(b) Sometimes the future indicative is used,
but never after ὅπως. Thus ἔσται in Heb. 3, 12.
Other tenses of the indicative are occasionally
found.

Exercise on Final or Purpose Clauses

Translate and re-translate :—

(1) Matt. 19, 13 : προσηνέχθησαν, 1st aor. pass.
of προσφέρω ; ἐπιθῇ, 2nd aor. subjunc. of ἐπιτίθημι ;
προσεύξηται, 1st aor. subjunc. of προσεύχομαι.

(2) John 17, 1-4 : for ἐλήλυθεν see ἔρχομαι. In all cases after ἵνα here the 1st aor. subjunc. is used.

(3) 1 Cor. 4, 6 : while μάθητε is 2nd aor. subjunc. (of μανθάνω) yet φυσιοῦσθε is pres. indic.

LESSON XXXIII

Some Rules of Syntax (*Continued*)

(e) THE INFINITIVE MOOD

This mood partakes of the character of both verb and noun. Hence it may itself be a subject or an object of another verb, or may have a subject or an object. See Lesson XV.

(1) For an example of the infinitive as the subject of a verb see Rom. 7, 18.

(2) For an example of the infinitive as an object see Phil. 2, 6, where εἶναι is used as a noun with the article τό, both being the object of ἡγήσατο.

(3) *When the subject of the infinitive is expressed it is always in the accusative case.* The English rendering is usually by a clause beginning with "that." Thus, in Acts 14, 19, νομίσαντες αὐτὸν τεθνηκέναι is, lit., "thinking him to have died," i.e., "thinking that he had died." In Luke 24, 23, οἱ λέγουσιν αὐτὸν ζῆν is, lit., "who say Him to live," i.e., "who say that He is alive."

But when the subject of the infinitive is the same as that of the preceding verb it is not expressed, except for emphasis, and any words in agreement with it are put in the nominative. Thus in Rom. 15, 24, ἐλπίζω διαπορευόμενος θεάσασθαι ὑμᾶς, I hope

216

passing through to see you, if the subject of
θεάσασθαι were expressed it would be με, but the
same person is the subject of both verbs, and hence
it is omitted and the participle agreeing is in the
nominative. Cp. Rom. 1, 22.

(4) The infinitive may be in various cases.
For the genitive see Luke 10, 19, where τοῦ
πατεῖν is, lit., "(power) of treading," i.e., " power
to tread." So in Acts 27, 20, where ἡμᾶς is the
acc. subject. In 2 Cor. 1, 8, there is an example
both of the acc. with the infin., and of the genit. of
the infin. The genitive often expresses purpose
(Matt. 2, 13 : 3, 13 : 21, 32), or even result
(Acts 7, 19).

For the dative see 2 Cor. 2, 13. Here τῷ . . .
εὑρεῖν is dative of cause " through (my not)
finding "; με is the acc. subject ; Τίτον is the
object.

(5) These cases of the infinitive often come after
prepositions. See Matt. 13, 5-6, where each διά
governs all that follows. In Matt. 24, 12, note
that τὴν ἀνομίαν is the subject of the infin. Cp.
Mark 5, 4. In Matt. 13, 25, the acc. with the
infinitive is governed by ἐν; in 26, 32, the article
with the acc. and infin. are all governed by μετά.
In Matt. 6, 1, αὐτοῖς is " by them."

(6) ὥστε with the infin., or with the acc. and
infin., expresses result. See Luke 9, 52, and Matt.
8, 24 : 13, 32 ; Acts 16, 26.

(7) The infinitive is occasionally used as an imperative (Phil. 3, 16, στοιχεῖν ; Rom. 12, 15).

(8) The negative with the infinitive may be either οὐ or μή ; οὐ denies as a matter of fact ; in all other cases and generally speaking μή is used. Note οὐδ᾽ (not μηδ᾽) in John 21, 25 ; οἶμαι is " I suppose," but the οὐ intimates the certainty that the world would not contain, etc.

Exercise on the Infinitive

Translate and re-translate :—

(1) 2 Cor. 10, 2 : τὸ μὴ . . . θαρρῆσαι, lit., "the not . . . to be bold " is the object of δέομαι ; παρὼν is nom. pres. partic. of πάρειμι.

(2) Acts 9, 3-4 : ἐγένετο is " it came to pass " (see γίνομαι) ; this is followed by the acc. with the infin. ; πεσὼν, aor. partic. of πίπτω.

(3) Luke 18, 1 : πρὸς τὸ δεῖν, lit., "unto the to be necessary " ; then follows the acc. with the infin., " them to pray," i.e., " that they ought always to pray."

(4) John 1, 48 : φωνῆσαι, 1st aor. infin. with Φίλιππον as subject and σε as object.

(5) 2 Cor. 8, 11 : ποιῆσαι, 1st aor. infin. ; ἐκ τοῦ ἔχειν, lit., " out of the having."

(6) Heb. 2, 8, and verse 15.

SYNTAX OF PARTICIPLES

(f) PARTICIPLES

These are verbal adjectives. Hence they agree with nouns expressed or understood.

(1) The present and perfect participles are often used with the verb "to be," making compound tense forms. See καιομένη ἦν, was burning, in Luke 24, 32 ; also Gal. 4, 24, "are allegorized." Literalism must not be pressed. Thus in Matt. 18, 20, εἰσιν . . . συνηγμένοι is not "are having been gathered together," but "are gathered together." In Luke 3, 23, ἦν . . . ἀρχόμενος is "was beginning (His ministry)," not "began to be (about thirty)."

(2) A participle may simply be an adjective as in τῇ ἐχομένῃ ἡμέρᾳ (Acts 21, 26), on the next day, where the verb is a partic. middle of ἔχω. So in 1 Tim. 1, 10, ὑγιαινούσῃ is "healthful," but is a present participle.

(3) The participle with the article is often equivalent to a noun : in 1 Thess. 1, 10, τὸν ῥυόμενον ἡμᾶς, lit. "the (One) delivering us," is "Our Deliverer." In Mark 4, 14, ὁ σπείρων is "the sower."

(4) The participle is frequently explanatory. Thus in Phil. 2, 7, λαβών explains the sentence "He emptied Himself" ; in verse 8 γενόμενος explains "He humbled Himself." In Rom. 12, 9, etc., the participles show how the command in verse 8 is to be carried out. So in 1 Pet. 2, 18, and

in 3, 1 and 7, the participles show the mode of the fulfilment of the commands in verse 17.

Exercise in Participles

Translate and re-translate :—

(1) Gal. 4, 8-9 : εἰδότες (see οἶδα) ; οὖσιν, dat., plur., masc., pres. partic. of εἰμί, to (those) not being gods.

(2) Acts 5, 4 : μένον, nom., sing., neut., pres. partic. of μένω, lit., " remaining (did it not remain to thee) ? " ; πραθὲν, nom., sing., neut., 2nd aor. partic. pass. of πιπράσκω.

(3) 1 Thess. 2, 14-16 : ἐπάθετε, 2nd aor. of πάσχω ; ἔφθασεν, 1st aor. of φθάνω.

LESSON XXXIV

ACCENTS

(1) The accents were used originally to give the correct pitch or tone to a syllable. There are three—the acute ('), the grave (`), the circumflex (ˉ). The acute stands only on one of the last three syllables of a word, the circumflex only on one of the last two, the grave only on the last. An accent is marked only on vowels; in diphthongs on the second vowel, as in οὕτως, οὖν. The acute and the grave are put after the aspirate or breathing, whether the rough breathing ('), as in ἕξω, or the soft breathing ('), as in ἔχω. The circumflex is put over the breathing, as in οὗτος.

(2) A word that has the acute on the last syllable, as in βασιλεύς, is called *oxytone* (sharp-toned). When the acute is on the last syllable but one (the penult), as in οὕτως, it is called *paroxytone*. When the acute is on the last but two (the antepenult), as in ἄνθρωπος, it is called *proparoxytone*. The antepenult, if accented, always has the acute.

(3) If the last syllable of a word contains a long vowel, the acute accent must be on the last or last but one, the circumflex on the last only. If, therefore, the last syllable of a proparoxytone

221

is lengthened by declension the accent is thrown forward, so that the word becomes paroxytone, e.g., ἄνθρωπος but ἀνθρώπων.

(4) When the circumflex comes on the last syllable, as in αὐτοῦ, it is called *perispomenon ;* when on the penult, as in οὗτος, it is called *properispomenon.* ' This pronoun .provides an example of the fact that a penult has the circumflex when it is long by *nature,* while the last syllable is short by nature. Otherwise, it takes the acute, e.g., λόγος. [A syllable is long by *nature* when it has a long vowel, e.g., τιμή, or a diphthong, e.g., κτείνω ; it is long by *position* when it is followed by two consonants, e.g., ἵσταντες, or by one of the double consonants, ζ (d and s), ξ (κ and s), ψ (p and s), e.g., ἰσόψυχος.]

(5) Final αι and οι are regarded as short in determining the accent, as in ἄνθρωποι, νῆσοι, but as long in the optative ; thus ποιήσοι (not ποιήσοι).

(6) Genitives in εως and εων from nouns in -ις and -υς of the third declension have the acute on the antepenult, e.g., πόλεως (genitive of πόλις), but βασιλέως (gen. of βασιλεύς). So with all in -εύς.

(7) An oxytone changes its acute to a grave accent before other words in the sentence, e.g., Θεὸς ἦν.

Contracted Syllables

(8) A contracted syllable is accented if either

of the original syllables had an accent. A contracted penult or antepenult is accented regularly. A contracted final syllable is circumflexed, e.g., τιμῶ, from τιμάω. But if the original word was oxytone the acute is retained, e.g., βεβώς, from βεβαώς. If neither of the original syllables had an accent the contracted form is accented without regard to the contraction. Thus τίμαε becomes τίμα.

Accents Regarding Enclitics and Proclitics

(9) An enclitic is a word which loses its accent and is pronounced as part of the preceding word. The following are enclitics :—(a) the indefinite pronoun τις in all its forms ; (b) the personal pronouns μοῦ, μοί, μέ, σοῦ, σοί, σέ ; (c) the pres. indic. of εἰμί (except the 2nd sing. εἶ) ; (d) φημί, φησίν, φασίν ; (e) the particles γε, τε, and the inseparable δε in ὅδε, etc. ; (f) the indefinite adverbs ποτέ, που, περ, πω, πως.

If a word is proparoxytone it receives from the enclitic an acute on the last syllable as a second accent, e.g., ἄνθρωπός τις, and so if a word is properispomenon, e.g., δεῖξόν μοι.

(10) Enclitics lose their accent when the preceding word is (a) oxytone, e.g., αὐτόν τινας (Mark 12, 13) ; (b) paroxytone, e.g., Ἰουδαίων τε (Acts 14, 1) ; (c) perispomenon, e.g., ἀγαπῶν με (John 14, 21).

(11) Enclitics retain their accent (a) if they

begin or end a sentence, e.g., φησίν in John 18, 29 ; (*b*) if they are dissyllables after a paroxytone (to avoid three successive unaccented syllables), e.g., λόγου ἐστίν (Jas. 1, 23) ; (*c*) when the preceding syllable is elided, e.g., δι' ἐμοῦ, John.14, 6 ; (*d*) if a dissyllable after a proclitic (see below), e.g., οὐκ εἰμί, John 3, 28 ; (*e*) the personal pronouns μοῦ, μοῖ, etc., keep their accent after an accented preposition, e.g., περὶ ἐμοῦ, John 15, 26 (except after πρός in πρός με, John 6, 65).

(12) Ἐστί (ἐστίν) at the beginning of a sentence retains its accent, and after οὐκ, μή, εἰ, καί, ἀλλά and τοῦτο, or a paroxytone syllable, e.g., Ἰουδαίων ἐστίν (John 4, 22), or in mild emphasis, e.g., νῦν ἐστίν (John 4, 23). Again, ἔστι, denoting existence or possibility, retains its accent, e.g., ἅγιον ἔστιν (Acts 19, 2).

(13) Some monosyllables have no accent, and are closely attached to the following word. They lose their accent in it. These are called *proclitics*. Such are the articles ὁ, ἡ, οἱ, αἱ, the prepositions εἰς, ἐξ (ἐκ), ἐν, the conjunctions εἰ and ὡς and the negative οὐ (οὐκ, οὐχ). But οὐ takes the acute when it stands alone, as οὔ, *no !* A proclitic followed by an enclitic is oxytoned, as οὔτις (which may be written as one word).

(14) Examples of change of words by accents : ἡ, the (fem.), ἤ, or, than, ἥ, who (fem.) ; τίς, who ? τις, someone ; οὐ, not, οὗ, where ; ποῦ, where ?, που, somewhere ; αὐται, they (fem. plur.), αὐταί, these (fem.).

ENGLISH INDEX

ENGLISH INDEX

GREEK INDEX

Note.—*This list is limited to certain particles, prepositions, pronouns, adjectives, etc., and a few irregular
verbs, all of frequent use and which receive special notice*